Praise for *A Min*
(the original edition of *..merica*)

"*It is only through a shift in consciousness that the world will be transformed. Congressman Tim Ryan has written a truly powerful book in which he shares a vision for the United States that reflects this ideal. He reminds us that the word 'United' in our country's name is first and foremost a spiritual principle. That we are all connected, that loving each other and working together as one is not for fanciful daydreamers—it is a real possibility. He writes eloquently of the power of kindness in how we interact with each other and more significantly how our government can implement mindfulness in its dealings with its citizens. As we become more enlightened, great political leaders will emerge from this new consciousness to lead us to Camelot, Avalon, or a Shining City on a Hill. Tim Ryan is one of those who can get us back to the 'United' in U.S.A., and we can, maybe for the first time, live our national motto, 'e pluribus unum.' Must reading for all.*"

— **Dr. Wayne W. Dyer**, best-selling author of *Wishes Fulfilled: Mastering the Art of Manifesting*

"*Visionary. Wise. And practical! This book is powerful medicine that can change your life and bring benefit to us all.*"

— **Dr. Jack Kornfield**, author of *A Path with Heart*

"*Congressman Ryan has written a book that explores the importance of being mindful and self-aware and the benefits of improved performance and reduced stress that follow. Perhaps, if more members of Congress were mindful of the moment, our country would be a better place.*"

— **Linda Sánchez**, United States congresswoman, California, co-author of *Dream in Color*

HEALING AMERICA

ALSO BY TIM RYAN

The Real Food Revolution

The above is available at your local bookstore,
or may be ordered by visiting:

Hay House USA: www.hayhouse.com®
Hay House Australia: www.hayhouse.com.au
Hay House UK: www.hayhouse.co.uk
Hay House India: www.hayhouse.co.in

HEALING AMERICA

*How a Simple Practice
Can Help Us Recapture
the American Spirit*

CONGRESSMAN
TIM RYAN

HAY HOUSE, INC.
Carlsbad, California • New York City
London • Sydney • New Delhi

Published in the United States by: Hay House, Inc.: www.hayhouse.com®
Published in Australia by: Hay House Australia Pty. Ltd.: www.hayhouse
.com.au • *Published in the United Kingdom by:* Hay House UK, Ltd.: www
.hayhouse.co.uk • *Published in India by:* Hay House Publishers India:
www.hayhouse.co.in

The information contained in this book is not intended to diagnose,
treat, prevent, or cure any disease, or to provide specific medical advice.
Questions about the relationship between nutrition, supplements,
meditative practices and your health should be directed to a qualified
health practitioner. The reader and associated health professionals
are responsible for evaluating the risks of any therapy reviewed in
this book. Those responsible made every effort possible to thoroughly
research the accuracy of the information and assume no responsibility
for errors, inaccuracies, or omissions.

**Library of Congress Cataloging-in-Publication Data
for the original edition**

Ryan, Tim, 1973-
    A mindful nation : how a simple practice can help us reduce stress,
improve performance, and recapture the American spirit / Tim Ryan.
      p. cm.
    ISBN 978-1-4019-3929-8 (hardback)
Mindfulness-based cognitive therapy--United States. 2. Self-reliance--
United States. I. Title.
  RC489.M55R93
  2012 616.89'1425--dc23

                                                      2011044970

Tradepaper ISBN: 978-1-4019-5588-5
e-book ISBN: 978-1-4019-5595-3

1st edition, March 2012
2nd edition, March 2013
3rd edition, September 2018

Printed in the United States of America

CONTENTS

*To Andrea, with deep gratitude
for all of your love,
all of the time.*

FOREWORD

This book is a remarkable and unusual gift to the world. It is remarkable in that it is written by a sitting politician who is advocating that we look deeply within ourselves to rediscover what is most trustworthy and most beautiful about us as a people—individually and collectively—and as a nation. It is unusual in that Congressman Ryan is pointing out a capability we all already have and showing us something that is not only possible but also potentially life transforming, and that is basically free.

At the same time, he is also asking something of us, and certainly of himself as well, namely, that we experiment with paying attention in a new way, and more deliberately. He is suggesting that *how* we pay attention, and not just *what* we pay attention to, can lead to significant changes in the quality of our lives, as well as to profound healing and transformation in our country. In an era in which the greater good often seems sidelined and diminished, and many feel a literal and metaphorical impoverishment and sense of disengagement, disempowerment, bewilderment, and profound loss regarding the state of our country, Congressman Ryan's message is simple, timely, inspired, and inspiring. It is also immanently practical. And it can be implemented immediately, by all of us, to one degree or another, and grow over time.

My work in mindfulness-based stress reduction (MBSR) began with a vision inspired in part by an important, even daring, government document: the Surgeon General's 1979 report, *Healthy People*. It called upon individual citizens to assume a greater degree of responsibility for their own and their family's health. It stated that no amount of money could address the negative consequences bound to emerge from unhealthy ways of living and not dealing effectively with life stresses. While at that time stress was not considered a risk factor for mortality and disease, many years later there is incontrovertible evidence that stress, if not dealt with effectively, can take years off our lives. There is also now evidence that meditative practices may be a very effective means of refining our response to stress and also of counteracting its damaging effects.

That same year, I set up a stress-reduction clinic at the University of Massachusetts Medical Center based entirely on training medical patients in a meditative practice known as *mindfulness*. It was an experiment in developing a model for a more participatory medicine and health care by taking an educational and public health approach—one which would recognize the powerful interior biological, psychological, and social resources of each individual medical patient and teach them how to mobilize those resources to enhance their own health and well-being. At the time, many people with chronic conditions were falling through the cracks of the health-care system. Today, those cracks have become chasms, and in spite of the health-care system's great technological advances, for the average American it falls far short of promoting genuine health and putting the patient at the center of health and healing.

It turns out that the most important resources people have for participating in their own health care are not found in technology. They are rather found in their natural capacity to pay attention and to cultivate awareness, and in a willingness to bring a modicum of kindheartedness and compassion to themselves and others. Systematically cultivating these capacities and making practical use of them in our everyday lives is what mindfulness is all about.

In his book, Congressman Ryan walks us through the simplicity and the relevance of such innate human capabilities, and shows why and how they can bring about positive changes in our society. He describes the people, the communities, and the research behind extremely promising initiatives unfolding in our country on many different levels, in many different circumstances, extending far beyond our current problems with health care.

Mindfulness can literally change our brains, improve our capacity for perspective taking and decision making, and enhance our emotional intelligence and our ability to act with clarity and wisdom, alone and in concert with others. It could also catalyze a renewed and authentic civility in public discourse. It proffers, in small but not insignificant ways, the possibility for our nation to wholeheartedly and authentically embody its deepest democratic principles and longings.

In January 2005, when *Coming to Our Senses* first came out, my publisher, Bob Miller, sent it to all 535 members of Congress. As it turns out, Congressman Ryan read the 100-page section on mindfulness and politics, and it was an impetus for his eventually attending the Power of Mindfulness retreat he describes in the book.

I first met Tim Ryan when he attended that retreat, in early November 2008. He had just been reelected to a fifth term, and instead of celebrating, here he was coming to a remote mountain valley for a week and immersing himself in a rigorous practice that from the outside looks a lot like nothing—just sitting and walking, mostly in silence, and following a set of simple instructions about how to pay attention to whatever is going on in one's experience moment by moment. He threw himself into the practice wholeheartedly. It was clear that he knew in some deep way what he was getting into and was making optimal use of the time we had there together. We stayed in touch afterward, and over time, as we became friends, I came to appreciate how deep his integrity and love for the people and potential of America are. This book is a testament to that integrity and that vision of our essential goodness as a people, and what might be possible for us as a nation in this ever more interdependent world.

As you will see, this book is a reflection of Tim Ryan's personal history and roots, and his deep and very personal commitment to this country, to his constituents, and ultimately, to all of us as Americans. He has researched his subject extensively—through his own mindfulness practice and by traveling around the country and speaking with some of the leading researchers and clinicians, educators, and military leaders who form the cutting edge of this new approach to being, learning, and doing. Throughout this odyssey, he finds himself reflecting on his vision for the country as he searches out the places in which mindfulness is being used to address some of the most compelling issues of our times. The book confronts head-on the tough and heartrending circumstances and conditions Congressman Ryan sees every day in his district. He makes a compelling case for the transformative potential of mindfulness in our personal lives and relationships, and in our institutions, whatever the circumstances are in which we find ourselves.

And who can argue, as he himself emphasizes, with training our children in the *how* of paying attention so that they can excel at learning, rather than just yelling at them to pay attention, which so often happens in our schools? Who can argue with encouraging and actually practicing pro-social behaviors such as kindness and compassion in both children and adults as a way to enrich and deepen our ability to relate effectively with others and improve our own quality of life? Who can argue with our need to slow down a bit and cultivate greater ease of being, to appreciate *how* we are in relationship with ourselves, with each other, with nature, and with the society we live in, in the face of the ever accelerating pressures and demands of our digitally driven era? Who can argue with confronting PTSD and suicide in the military, and taking care of our troops and their families in ways that are up to the tasks and burdens that they shoulder?

The list of societal, economic, and political spheres in which mindfulness can make a profound difference for a relatively modest investment goes on. And so does the momentum of research in these areas, as Tim Ryan makes clear in his conversations with many of the leaders of what he terms "this quiet revolution."

This book is not based on wishful thinking or on pie-in-the-sky romanticism and idealism. The shift in consciousness that mindfulness involves really is a radical act in the sense of going to the very root of our problems with suffering and its human causes. That may be exactly why it is so valuable and potentially powerful: because it calls us to inhabit and exercise the deepest dimensions of our own being and our own multiple intelligences as human beings, moment by moment by moment. It is something we are all capable of.

The developments that Congressman Ryan is pointing out are already flowering across our country, in some of our most august institutions, and in some of our most stressed. They are flowering not because they are easy to implement—although often they *are* relatively easy to implement—but because they are absolutely necessary. Mindfulness is not a matter of left or right, Republican or Democrat, liberal or conservative. It is not a matter of race or class or gender, although societal differences and inequities matter and need to be recognized and addressed. Ultimately, it is about being human, pure and simple. It is about being alive, and knowing it. It is about doing the right thing for the right reasons because our own well-being and the health of our nation hang in the balance. As I have heard Tim Ryan say, cultivating mindfulness is akin to boosting the immune system of the country from the inside. And since there is no one right way to cultivate and deepen our capacity for mindfulness, each one of us could influence the world by taking a degree of personal responsibility for developing our own unique ways to embody mindful awareness. That may well be one of the most profound ways we can contribute to the well-being of the larger society and the planet itself. It's a process that could begin with reading this book and reflecting on what it touches within you.

Just naming what might be possible—a mindful nation—and offering a vibrant vision for this country at a moment when it is longing for a greater sense of clarity and common purpose, may inspire each of us to imagine what our unique contributions to such a vision might be. For this, we have Tim Ryan to thank. He is the first, and I hope not the last, to see and articulate this perspective and champion its implementation in the political arena. It is only a start. But a step in the right direction is just what we need, a place to begin, with a vision that embodies integrity and spaciousness, big enough to include all Americans.

Instead of losing our minds just when we need them the most, with the help of mindfulness we can integrate all the dimensions of our experience—emotional, somatic, cognitive, and social. Rather than *black or white, this or that, us or them* modes of thinking, the cultivation of mindfulness can naturally lead us to greater clarity, especially in the face of very complex systems and rapidly changing circumstances. It helps us discern wise, effective, outside-the-box, long-lasting solutions to real problems.

Tim Ryan shows us a way that is continually unfolding and which promises not a utopian end point but a way of being that could well serve our deepest needs and aspirations as a nation for generations to come. He is encouraging all of us to find and cultivate our innate capacity for mindfulness, in whatever ways we are most drawn to. He is encouraging us to explore how it can be cultivated within our lives, our families, and our communities. The potential benefits are endless if we can begin paying attention to what is most important and closest to home for us, learning from this gesture of wakefulness and presence, and acting on what we learn. This is an adventure that can speak to all of us, and can elevate our society in countless ways.

Jon Kabat-Zinn
Lexington, Massachusetts
October 2011

PREFACE

When I wrote this book six years ago, I wanted to help people see that if we take a little time each day for quiet, over time we will begin to bring our stress and anxiety levels down. We'll be able to be more present, more composed, and kinder to both ourselves and others. We'll learn to *respond* thoughtfully to our daily challenges instead of simply *react* to them. I wrote it because I knew that most Americans wanted to reduce their anxiety but just didn't quite know *how*. Mindfulness can be a part of the *how-to* for many people, regardless of whatever beliefs they may hold. I wrote this book because I know how much we encourage our kids (often with raised voices) to pay attention. Simple mindfulness practices are one way of teaching them *how* to focus and pay attention and of setting an example of doing so.

I also wrote this book because I know that as we make a discipline of being more mindful, we can begin to see that we really are connected deeply to each other. That we are—as I was taught from a young age—our brother's and sister's keeper. That merely by being citizens of the same country, we have an obligation to look out for each other and make sure everyone has an opportunity to reach their full potential. I wanted people to experience that by taking some time to pay attention, on purpose, we can help heal our bodies, minds, and spirits too. And that when this "paying attention on purpose" is brought into the national systems that treat our wounded warriors and their families, try to heal our sick, and educate our youth, it could transform the old systems and inject them with new energy and awareness: a healing and creative energy that will allow us to meet the huge challenges we face as citizens of the United States, of the globe, and as a species. That was my hope.

While we have made some strides in bringing contemplative and complementary practices to the broader society and have the studies to show its manifold benefits, things have gotten progressively worse. We are hurting more now than we were then, which is why I've decided to convey the urgency I feel by updating the title from *A Mindful Nation* to *Healing America*. Since the book's original release, we have seen an increase in "noise" in our society: more screen time for our kids, more texting, more news alerts, more media outlets, more vitriol on social media, more distractions, more divisions, and a general unease about where we are and where we are going. We have work to do on the road to becoming a more mindful nation.

In our politics, our economy, and our culture, we have all become more uneasy, to say the least. In the original book, I spoke about "anger lurking on the fringes." Today, it's front and center in our public discourse. We are separating ourselves into the red team and blue team and ignoring the basic spiritual principle that we are all unified at a deep level. We're all on the human team. We are going to have some honest disagreements. In a democracy, we *need* to have honest disagreements, but the other people are not your enemy. They are your fellow citizens. That is easy to forget but essential to remember. *E pluribus unum*: out of many, one.

As I travel this country, I hear it all the time from people who are white, black, brown, gay, and straight. People from the North, South, West, or Midwest—all are feeling the national temperature go up. They are also feeling their personal stress levels rise as a result of their inability to gain stability in their own lives. In the midst of all the noise and confusion, our inability to find the focused attention we need in order to creatively take on these challenges frustrates us further. We all seem to be in the middle of a personal energy crisis.

Many citizens see that reduced economic opportunities and stagnant wages have trapped people in an outmoded economic system, and they have no idea how to break out. Globalization continues to leave more and more people behind, and if we don't play our cards right, computerized systems, robotics, and machine learning will leave even more people failing to make a living wage. Millions of families—many of them African American— find themselves the victims of a broken criminal justice system that is often unjust to people of color. Large numbers of undocumented workers are trapped in an immigration system that is based on fear and anger instead of hope and opportunity. We're in the middle of an opioid crisis of mammoth proportions: we lost more people to overdose deaths in 2016 than we lost in combat during the entire Vietnam War. Half of our country has either diabetes or prediabetes. For all of these reasons and more, we are in a time of great national anxiety.

My hope in reintroducing this book to the American people is to showcase very effective ways we can deal with that pressure by applying healthy approaches that don't cost a lot of money and don't carry damaging side effects. Let's each help bring the national political temperature down so we can begin to concentrate on solving these huge challenges that face us as a people. If each of us learns how to better reduce our own stress levels, become less reactive and judgmental, and be kinder to ourselves and others, that will naturally reduce the stress of the country.

Finally, I want everyone to know that this is not a journey outward to go get something we don't have. This isn't the moon shot. It's the *you* shot. This is a journey inward to rediscover the beauty and profound capabilities you already have. It's an inward adventure that helps you see the deep reservoir of resiliency you have been blessed with—a resiliency that is essential for the long national journey we need to embark upon.

I offer this book to you so you can see that by taking a mindfulness journey, slowing down and paying attention on purpose, you can begin the healing process for your own body, mind, and spirit and help bring healing and renewed energy to our body politic.

INTRODUCTION

A quiet revolution is happening in America. It's not a revolution fueled by anger lurking on the fringes of our democracy. It's a peaceful revolution, being led by ordinary citizens: teachers in our public schools; nurses and doctors in hectic emergency rooms, clinics, and hospitals; counselors and social workers in tough neighborhoods; military leaders in the midst of challenging conflicts; and many others across our nation. This revolution is supported by the work of scientists and researchers from some of the most prominent colleges and universities in America, such as the University of Wisconsin, Stanford, UCLA, the University of Miami, Emory, Duke, and Harvard, to name just a few.

At the core of this revolution is mindfulness.

Put simply, mindfulness is about finding ways to slow down and pay attention to the present moment—which improves performance and reduces stress. It's about having the time and space to attend to what's right in front of us, even though many other forces are trying to keep us stuck in the past or are inviting us to fantasize or worry about the future. It's about a natural quality each of us possesses and that we can further develop in just a few minutes a day.

I started a daily mindfulness practice a few years ago and immediately began to appreciate its practical benefits in my everyday life. It quiets the mind. It helps you harness more of your energy. It increases your focus and allows you to relax and pay better attention to what you're doing and to those around you. My football coaches would have loved it. It's the kind of performance enhancer any athlete would be eager to have. And it's definitely all natural.

Like many who have tasted the benefits of increased focus, decreased stress, and a quieter mind, I was motivated to share it with my family and friends. Given my work as a United States congressman, I was also motivated to see its benefits shared on a much larger scale. I recognized its potential to help transform core institutions in America—schools, hospitals, the military, and social services. I felt that this simple practice could help my constituents face the many stressful challenges of daily life: the pain of war. Economic insecurity. The frustrations of being sick or taking care of sick relatives in a broken health-care system. The challenge of teaching children to pay attention and be kind to themselves and others as they swim in a world of distraction and aggression.

I wrote this book to promote the values of slowing down, taking care of ourselves, being kind, and helping each other. It seems to me that if we embrace these values individually, it will benefit us collectively. And our country will be a little bit better off as a result. We don't need a new set of values. I really believe that we can reinvigorate our traditional, commonly held American values—such as self-reliance, perseverance, pragmatism, and taking care of each other—by adding a little more mindfulness to our lives. The people you will meet in this book have a collective and powerful vision for America. And it's contagious because it's based on a deep concern for the well-being of their fellow men and women. Their research and innovative approaches provide us not just with hope for a better world but with an alternative vision that moves us forward—together. The evidence I've seen tells me that the approaches described in this book can provide more effective results than many other more costly programs. If more citizens can reduce stress and increase performance—even if only by a little—they will be healthier and more resilient. They will be better equipped to face the challenges of daily life and arrive at creative solutions to the challenges facing our nation.

⌇

I start this book by acknowledging the many difficulties we face in our country today—economic struggles, lack of opportunity, divisiveness, daunting environmental and energy challenges. Is it any wonder that the courageous spirit of America and faith in our cherished values of self-reliance and stick-to-itiveness have flagged? Cultivating mindfulness can help revive this kind of spirit, so we can pursue our aims with renewed vigor. For each one of us, it can put a little lift in our step, and when that happens for more and more people, it can amount to real societal change.

I came to this view through my own experience of discovering the value of mindfulness and how it's been helping me in my life, which I describe in Chapter 2. But I don't want you to just take my word for it, so I recount in Chapter 3 what researchers at major institutions studying mindfulness, awareness, kindness, and compassion are finding out about how and why it works—and what it can do for us. Talking to them helped me see how relevant mindfulness practice can be to everyday concerns like stress, persistent bad moods, burnout, and poor performance—for our students, teachers, health-care practitioners and patients, soldiers and other uniformed personnel, and many others.

Mindfulness is indeed making inroads in our schools, our health-care systems, and our military. In Chapters 4, 5, and 6, I report on firsthand experiences and conversations with key people working in these areas that are so vital to the health of our country. It's incredibly moving to see children finding ways to become happier and better at learning, teachers discovering ways to have a better classroom atmosphere and finding renewed inspiration in their work, health-care providers developing low-cost means to improve their patients' health and increase self-care while decreasing burnout and improving bedside manner, our troops and police and firefighters learning to perform better and with more awareness and intelligence, and our veterans receiving highly effective care for the stress and trauma they bring home with them. I firmly believe these applications are improving lives at lower cost than many other less effective methods.

We face huge challenges in our economy, our environment, and our energy systems. Mindfulness and awareness may help us tackle them, as I discuss in Chapter 7. Of course, mindfulness is not a cure-all for our most pressing problems. It may, in fact, seem like a very small thing pitted against a behemoth. And yet lots of little things here and there can lead to systemic change. The age of oil—which has shaped our current economy and our energy network, and delivered us our tallest environmental challenges—began as a little well here and a little well there, and before you knew it, a whole new system was born. The same can happen again with the innovative approaches springing up in the intellectual wells of our nation. As recent presidents have emphasized, our problems are interconnected. Seeing them as a whole leads to better, more sustainable solutions.

I conclude this book by envisioning in Chapter 8 what our nation could look like when we recapture the American spirit embodied in our traditional values of self-reliance, frugality, innovation, and getting the job done—with a little help from our own innate mindfulness. The mindfulness revolution is not quite as dramatic as the moon shot or the civil rights movement, but I believe that in the long run, it can have just as great an impact.

The kind of practice I've been doing is a classic mindfulness meditation, which relies on sitting in an upright yet relaxed posture for a period of time and paying attention to your breathing, your bodily sensations, and your environment. This practice has been demonstrated to provide measurable benefits in health and well-being. It's helped many people with anxiety, depression, and stress—both the everyday levels of stress and the crippling levels of stress that send people to the hospital.

I am not a mindfulness teacher. There are plenty of great teachers, books, workshops, and organizations to provide guidance. In the Afterword, you will find a simple mindfulness instruction written by Dr. Susan Bauer-Wu, a nursing educator who helps caregivers and patients learn mindfulness in order to reduce the stress of their jobs and decrease the difficulties they may be having with their health. At the ends of Chapters 1 through 7, I include suggestions for what you can do to bring more mindfulness into your own life and your own community. And at the end of the book, there are lists of resources that will help you locate people and organizations that can assist you in bringing more mindfulness into your world.

In my last year at John F. Kennedy High School in Warren, Ohio, we all took a class called Senior Service. We had to participate in a program to assist someone in need, by going out to places like nursing homes and elementary schools. It was a way for us to put our core values into action. Our natural compassion and kindness were meant to be shared to help make the world a better place. It's in that spirit that I wrote this book.

As a political leader, I know that to make the world a better place we need practical applications that have been tried and tested. And when I find applications that work, I like to let people know about them. I believe I would be derelict in my duty as a congressman if I didn't do my part to make mindfulness accessible to as many people as possible in our nation.

CHAPTER 1

YOU CAN GET
THERE FROM HERE

In a crisis, be aware of the danger—
but recognize the opportunity.

— JOHN F. KENNEDY

America has always been defined by how we have
responded to crises. The founders of our country rallied
the separate colonies in a unified response to a government that no longer cared about the governed. Following
the Civil War, we persevered through a long period of
holding the country together after it had been torn apart,
and progressives resolve to this day to deliver fully on
the promise of civil rights for all. After the stock market
collapse of 1929 and the Great Depression that followed,
America united behind a philosophy that understood
that we are all in this together. Our citizens knew in a
deep way that surviving and thriving are best achieved
when individuals, families, and communities are working
in concert for the betterment of everyone.

After Pearl Harbor, the country united once again.
Each citizen rose to the occasion and did what had to

be done to protect the values we hold dear. Millions of women in my grandmother's generation answered the call and entered the workforce. They brought their talents and skills out of the home and into the world of commerce. They forever changed the American workforce, and broadened and enhanced the role of women in our society. The women of America turned a crisis into an opportunity.

Out of the struggles our citizens endured during the first half of the 1900s, they developed an inner resiliency that became the engine for the economic, political, and social progress that defined America in the 20th century. During the Depression, my great-grandfather walked a couple of miles every morning to the local steel mill to see if they were hiring any workers. Along with hundreds of others, my great-grandpa hoped he would be one of the few to get picked, even if just for a few hours of work. He was rarely selected. Nonetheless, he made that walk every day, month after month.

My great-grandfather, the millions of working women, the soldiers who served our country—all Americans developed a tenacity and resiliency during difficult times. The trials united us. And as we made it out the other side of those trying times, we were a stronger, more resilient country. The outer strength of our country was a reflection of the inner strength of its citizens.

We witnessed examples of this inner courage in the days after 9/11. The country was operating from our natural instinct for compassion. We were acting from the heart, and we all were touched by the selflessness of others we saw on the news: the first responders sacrificing their own lives by running into burning buildings while everyone else was running out; New Yorkers waiting in long lines to donate blood for the injured; the thousands of caregivers who voluntarily came to Ground Zero from all over the country and risked their personal health to help the victims. These were all marvelous acts of human kindness. Unfortunately, after several weeks, we succumbed to fearmongering. We stopped following our hearts and the example of earlier generations. We reverted to focusing on what divides us as a country. And this division adds to our anxiety because we know, intuitively and through the lessons of history, that Lincoln was right: "A house divided against itself cannot stand."

When I was growing up in Niles, Ohio—which is five miles from where I live today when I'm not in Washington—I was taught by my first-generation Italian American grandparents, John and Ann Rizzi, that helping each other and working together to make a better community were what America was all about. After my grandparents died, I helped my mom clean out their house and stumbled across a tattered little book in the attic. I saw a column of names recorded month after month with the figure "$1.00" written after most of the names. I asked my mother what it was all about, and she told me that it was a record of the monthly dues that the immigrants who moved to Niles from Valsinni, Italy, paid into a mutual-aid fund administered by my great-grandfather. When anyone needed a helping hand, the group was there to provide it. My grandparents lived and breathed these values. They would say a rosary for someone in need, and my grandfather would bring them a pot of soup my grandmother had made. When his brother-in-law, my uncle Phil, was gravely ill, Grandpa dropped everything to spend each day doing whatever was needed. My cousins still cry when they think of it. Grandpa was totally involved in our lives; he was there for us—every game, every school function, every crisis. He taught us dignity and grace, and to be grateful for whatever we had and to always extend a hand to others. Yes, these were values within our ethnic community, but they were and are values common to all Americans, regardless of ancestry or how long they have been Americans. In my work—and in this book—I celebrate these values using many different words and phrases:

- Self-reliance
- Stick-to-itiveness
- Persistence
- Perseverance
- Diligence
- Hard work
- Getting
  the job done
- Innovation
- Resilience
- Thrift

- Frugality
- Practicality
- Pragmatism
- Caring
- Connection
- Community
- Mutual respect
- Taking care of
  each other
- Kindness
- Compassion

These values brought enormous power to the United States. But it seems we have foolishly wasted a lot of that power. "I hope our wisdom will grow with our power," Thomas Jefferson said, "and teach us that the less we use our power the greater it will be." Now, our wisdom has waned and it's taking our power with it. It is our responsibility to meet the high standard that Jefferson set for us.

When the same kindness and togetherness and diligence I saw in my grandparents emerged on 9/11, many of us were proud to be American and felt united as citizens, even in the midst of our fear. We put our arms around complete strangers as we watched events unfold on TVs in airports and department store windows. We let ourselves cry together in public.

But in the weeks and months afterward we rapidly returned to focusing on our differences, and those

differences seemed to become even starker. Both personally and publicly, we allowed ourselves to get wedged into
attitudes and beliefs that have made us smaller and held
us back. As the Homeland Security threat level entered
our lives on a daily basis, fear and desperation to fix
things once and for all took over.

⌒

Our attempts to fix our outer world have not made
us feel much safer or more secure, however. For the past
decade, we have been constantly reminded that we are
engaged in two wars. Our military men and women,
and their families—from thousands of communities
across America—have made enormous sacrifices. Many
of our troops have served gallantly in three or more
tours of duty. Their families are under great emotional
and financial pressure. The troops carry deep pain as
well. Many veterans return to our communities without
limbs. Others return with less visible signs of damage—
posttraumatic stress, depression, traumatic brain injury.
The suicide rate for veterans—which the Veterans
Administration estimated in 2010 to be some 120 per
week—is double the rate of the general populace. Troops
on active duty are also taking their lives. In July 2011, 33
soldiers committed suicide. Since 2010, an average of one
soldier a day has committed suicide.

Between Thanksgiving and Christmas in 2010, I visited the parents of a young soldier from my district who
had committed suicide. They lived in a quaint country
home with two or three open acres in the back that eventually abutted a forest with trails. The grass was particularly
green after a rainfall and the sky a deep blue, a gorgeous
Ohio day. They greeted me in the driveway and invited

me inside for a cup of coffee. We sat by a wood-burning stove as they talked about their son, what he was like as a boy, how funny he was and how much everyone loved him. I could feel the lump growing in my throat and my eyes beginning to well with tears. They told me about his girlfriend, some of the problems he had with the Veterans Administration, and the challenges of finding work. After an hour or so, we hugged, and I offered any help I could give them. As we walked to my car, the father pointed to a place in their backyard a hundred yards or so away from the house. Staring, he said, "That's where he did it. He walked back there as I stood here working." He paused to gather himself. "Then I heard the gun go off." There was a long silence. "I had no idea he was that upset." This family's pain was not going away anytime soon, probably never. Tragedies like this have left their mark in communities all across America.

～

No one needs to remind us that we are living through tough economic times as well. The wages of the middle class have been stagnant for over 30 years. The bright promise that a wave of high-tech jobs would greet college graduates upon their entry into the workforce and revive the middle class has now proven hollow. Meanwhile, workers continue to be replaced by labor-saving technology as hundreds of thousands of jobs have moved overseas. When my cousin Donny lost his job at Delphi, the huge automotive parts conglomerate that started out in Warren, Ohio, as Packard Electric (an arm of the Packard Motor Car Company), his last task was to unbolt the machines from the floor and pack them for shipment to China. Old industrial towns I represent in Congress—Niles, Akron, Warren, Youngstown—have experienced chronic unemployment for more than three decades, and the worldwide financial collapse occasioned by the subprime mortgage crisis hasn't helped. Thousands of families are underwater on their mortgages while global banks received a bailout—whether it was necessary or not. These families see CEOs getting golden parachutes and huge bonuses and tax cuts. According to former labor secretary Robert Reich, CEOs in the late 1960s earned 48 times what their employees were making. In 2010, they were making 325 times what their workers were earning. We have seen a huge transfer of wealth from the middle class to the wealthiest one percent. In 1980, the top one percent accounted for 12 percent of real income. As of 2014, they accounted for 20 percent. One-fifth of the income in our country is earned by just 1/100th of the people, and that group earns 81 times more than 50 percent of our citizens. The vast majority of Americans are working harder and longer, making less, and falling further and further behind. The cost of the most vital things we spend our money on— education, health care, and energy—has been increasing many times faster than the rate of inflation. The few who are prospering are celebrated in magazines and on talk shows, giving the false impression that America is still a land of milk and honey. But a much larger number are not prospering, and many are in dire straits. When you ask how the country *as a whole* is doing, the answer is "not so good." The once famous American middle class, the bedrock of our democracy, is disappearing while the media distract us with "reality" TV, shock jocks, and rants delivered by talking heads.

Are you okay with that?

I'm not okay with that.

America's challenges today stem from long-term systemic problems. They will not be solved with a legislative silver bullet created in Washington or our state capitols. Clearly we need a new direction. Our current thinking has caused millions of people to lose their jobs, their health care, their pensions, and their dignity. The present systems have told people to work hard and play by the rules and they will be rewarded. But when they get close to retirement, their benefits are often suddenly and callously stripped away. If a company goes bankrupt, the worker's family is the last in line to get made whole, behind the banks, creditors, and everyone else.

No one is immune; both blue-collar and white-collar workers are affected. I know, because I have been through these bankruptcies and plant closings with thousands of families in my congressional district. It is those families that motivate me to bring about change in this country at a deep, fundamental level. My experience tells me that tinkering at the edges is not enough. Just look around.

The U.S. Department of Agriculture recently reported that 12.3 percent of households in America face a daily risk of hunger, or "food insecurity." Many people, whether they have health insurance or not, agonize over what they would do if one of their children needed treatment for cancer, Down syndrome, or diabetes. Folks who have lost their jobs fear they will not be able to find another that pays as well. They grow anxious thinking that their dream of sending their son or daughter to college will be beyond their reach. I meet people all the time who are trying to support both their children and their parents on an income that is barely sufficient for themselves. Sixty-six million Americans are serving as "family caregivers"— taking care of a chronically ill family member, usually because they can't afford outside support. People under such circumstances are bundles of stress, and they break down in front of me when they talk about their plight.

Unfortunately, in many parts of our country, this economic anxiety is the norm, not the exception. Our household debt-to-disposable income ratio in 1952 was 38 percent. In 2011, it reached 112 percent. The average American household today owes approximately $137,000.

⌣

People are maxed out, squeezed, and crunched. They are running harder on an economic treadmill that just keeps getting faster and steeper. If someone asks us how we're doing, we may smile and say okay, but many of us are mentally and physically exhausted. We feel like we cannot get ahead. The American Dream is becoming a nightmare for more people each year. Is it any wonder our elections have been so volatile?

In my first couple of Appropriations Committee hearings a few years ago, I was startled when I heard our national trends outlined by experts in business and government. If we did not improve our education system, they said, this generation of students would be the first to be worse off than their parents. If we did not deal with the results of less healthy lifestyles, especially obesity, this would be the first generation of Americans to have a shorter life expectancy than their parents. We've also become a more wasteful country. Only a hundred years ago, we produced barely any garbage. We were frugal and squeezed whatever we could out of whatever we had. Now it has been estimated that 40 percent of all the edible food we produce ends up in a landfill—and the energy expended in growing, harvesting, processing, transporting, and refrigerating goes along with it, increasing our production of greenhouse gases and exacerbating our energy dependence. More than a quarter of the fresh water we use goes to produce food that *no one will ever eat*. We're depleting our God-given natural resources at an alarming rate.

Our brightest minds are not being enlisted to come up with innovative solutions to these tricky problems. A disproportionate number of our best graduates are drawn into jobs in finance, where it is estimated they are paid two to three times more than they would be in other industries. As Amy Binder reported in *Washington Monthly* in 2014, only 3.5 percent of Harvard grads go into government, 5 percent into health-related fields, 8.8 percent into public service in some form, while 31 percent took jobs in finance. But financial innovation has not served us well, as we saw when the fallout from ill-considered mortgages brought the world's financial system to its knees. Instead of an economic system that rewards craftsmanship, high manufacturing standards, and excellence in the skilled trades, we reward clever tricks and stratagems.

We are not in good shape. If our country were an alcoholic, we would be bottomed out and headed to rehab. We must do better than this. And I believe we can. We have the wherewithal, the talent, the ingenuity, and the capacity to address these challenges—but we won't do it by following the same paths that got us here. Is it sane to keep pursuing the same pathways thinking they will bring a different result? We need to take the advice from the doctor in the old Henny Youngman joke:

Patient: It hurts when I do this.
Doctor: Stop doing that.

We need to stop following the same old habits and patterns that have us stuck in a rut. We need new approaches that can draw out our deep inner resources. Once we learn to tap into these resources, we will find the strength to replenish, reform, and renew our country. For decades we believed that if we produced more, made more money, got the bigger house and the second car, we would be happy. The "pursuit of happiness" is enshrined in the Declaration of Independence, the founding document of our nation, and yet America as a whole is far from a happy place right now.

～

We can do much better. We can respond better to crises than we have before. At a deep level, we are more resilient than we know. We are much more powerful and creative than our current state of affairs would suggest. Strip away the materialism, the marketing, the media, and the technology, and our fundamental nature is revealed. You see what was displayed when people pulled together and helped each other out on 9/11: you see courage, confidence, and generosity, all the best qualities that are the essence of being an American—indeed, of being human. We are fundamentally good. Our basic nature is not unadulterated self-indulgence and consumption. Our spirit is not violent. Our soul does not desire that we get rich by any means necessary. The deepest part of who we are is not at peace with all the suffering in the world and the systems that perpetuate it. We all wince when we see someone suffering in our midst or even on the computer or television screen. When we hear the news of a shooting spree in a public place, we feel not only terror, but genuine compassion and concern.

I want Americans to act with the energetic generosity of spirit they showed on 9/11. I want *that* behavior to be the ethic of society today. Let's get rid of the phony concept of an America based on materialism, consumerism, and looking out for number one, where financial chicanery is our proudest accomplishment to show the world. There is no honor in that way of life, and no dignity in the idea that anything worthwhile has to be purchased.

It shouldn't be all that difficult to get us to move beyond this ethos, given how unhappy Americans have become. If we slow down and find some space away from the daily chatter that tells us how to think, who to be, and what to buy, we can discover our capacity for resilience. We can discover that the values that made this country great—self-reliance, diligence, community—are contained within each of us. We've tapped into them during great crises and revealed the best of who we are. And we can do it again—not just amid disasters but all the time.

Complex systemic problems cannot be solved by any one segment of our society—by public officials, experts, professionals, or pundits. We need everyone working together. As Reverend Jim Wallis, founder of *Sojourners* magazine and a passionate evangelical advocate for a new political order, has said, "We don't need to go further to the left or further to the right. We all need to go deeper." We need everyone committed to growing and developing themselves to their full potential. Much of our talent in this country goes untapped and undeveloped. It sits on the sidelines, or is pushed there, because of fear, doubt, and suffering. In the words of President Franklin D. Roosevelt, "The only limit to our realization of tomorrow will be our doubts of today."

We need to shake our doubt and reclaim the freedom that is our highest American value, our birthright. For a worker who has lost a job, this may mean going back to school, getting retrained, or starting a business; and I do believe the government has some role in helping that worker and supporting his or her family by ensuring access to health care and good education. America has a great opportunity to once more create a world-class skilled workforce and to develop high-end products and ship them to huge, growing markets in Asia. But we cannot do this if our workers doubt their own abilities to get retrained or succeed in school. We have no time left for doubt. We are falling behind. And America will only reduce its collective doubt if each individual citizen lessens his or her own doubt. As President Obama said in the State of the Union address in January 2011 in celebrating innovation as one of our core values, in America "we do big things." And when we've done big things, like establishing land-grant colleges or giving veterans an education through the GI bill, we took bold steps in response to the circumstances of the day. We adapted. We mobilized. We innovated.[1]

If we feel—in the speed and chaos of day-to-day living—we have lost our sense of purpose, then we need to learn how to come to that chaos with more awareness and more control over how we respond to it. Sometimes when we drive to work or to the store, we've been in such a distracted rush we can't even remember that the trip took place. *How did I get here?* We are missing precious moments with our children and our families, and the stress is taking its toll on our health.

If we want to *experience* happiness, and not just pursue it, we need to do what President Kennedy told us to do when we wanted peace with the Soviet Union: "begin by looking inward—by examining [our] own attitude toward the possibilities of peace." The self-examination

President Kennedy spoke of is a call to develop our inner resources—to develop skills that increase our awareness and understanding of our own thoughts, feelings, attitudes, fears, and beliefs. We all know that happiness is not something we can purchase. Happiness is found by deeply experiencing the exact moment we are in. Happiness is being totally alive. Obsessing about the future and worrying about the past rip us out of the only place where we can find true happiness: the present moment. But how do we find it?

We find the present moment in the midst of
our everyday lives. It's right in front of us.

People say our daughter, Isabella, is a girly girl. As a six-year-old, she loved dressing in cute outfits, putting on lip gloss, and bebopping around with her American Girl doll. She's smart and gets all As, but she shies away from physical contact and doesn't take much to sports. I went along with my wife, Andrea, to Isabella's and her brother Mason's first tae kwon do class. I was pretty sure Mason would love it because he also loves football and imitating a ninja. He roughhouses and wrestles and tackles. He just needed to taste the real practice of martial arts and he would love it.

I wasn't so sure about Bella. Her mother was aware that she might not like tae kwon do, but she wanted both her children to learn the respect, discipline, and effort that are inherent in this traditional Asian practice. If it didn't work for Bella, it didn't work for her.

Surprisingly, Bella took to it as much as Mason did. During the first practice, it blew my mind as she screamed at the top of her lungs and kicked the bag. The students kicked and punched the bags again and again to develop endurance and focus. They were taught to bow to show mutual respect each time they entered and exited the studio. Before they could pick up a piece of equipment, they had to wait for someone to offer it to them rather than simply grabbing it on their own. *This is teaching them great life skills,* I thought, *things parents so often just lecture children about but don't do themselves.* After the first class, Mason and Bella both wanted to continue and commit to at least two classes a week. It lifted my spirits to see these young children's minds acquiring some healthy discipline under the guidance of adult mentors. As a high school student, I had loved the guidance and support I got from my football coaches. The tae kwon do class offered Bella all of that and more.

A few weeks later, Bella and Mason were at home before going to tae kwon do practice. Andrea told me that they were playing the memory game. The children pay close attention to whatever sign or symbol or number comes up, and then recall and repeat it later. After struggling for a while, Bella said, "Mama, can we finish the game later? I'll be able to concentrate better after tae kwon do." When I heard that she had said that, it really struck me. This six-year-old can feel a difference in the way her mind works after practicing a martial art. She is cultivating the capacity to know what she is feeling and thinking, and what conditions can affect how she is feeling and thinking. After just a few weeks of training, Bella could already see how tae kwon do improved her concentration and focus. She also was aware enough of her current state of mind that she could better decide what activities were good for her to do at particular times. That's wisdom, an innate and essential part of being *fully* human. Parents all over the country are already sending kids to martial arts classes by the hundreds of thousands. And what are they learning? Hard work, resilience, relaxation, mutual respect, and how to pay attention to what's going on in their bodies and minds. They are learning a method that draws on the very ability that I think we need the most in these difficult times: mindfulness. And I think that ability can help draw from us those good old-fashioned American values that we need to carry us through these trying times.

Although it may seem like an unusual way to approach serious practical problems, I am convinced that our capacity to be *mindful* is the natural pathway to addressing so many of the difficulties we face. What is mindfulness? Mindfulness means being relaxed and aware of what's going on in our own minds. It means calmly paying attention to what we are doing, without being pulled into regrets about the past or fantasies of the future. It's our capacity to simply fully focus on what we're doing and make choices based on awareness of what's going on inside us and around us This innate human ability is the essence of composure and the source of high performance. We often let our presence of mind deteriorate and fall into patterns that are not healthy for ourselves and those around us; but we can always regain our mindfulness in a moment.

Our innate mindfulness has been likened to our sense of balance. We always have it, but we can stumble and lose our balance, and even fall. For example, when we play sports or dance, we can get off-balance, but we quickly regain our balance and reestablish ourselves. And we can develop and cultivate a stronger sense of balance through practice. In just the same way, we can become distracted by obsessive thoughts, worry, and fear. We're jittery and agitated, ill at ease. And yet, our mindfulness is just around the corner waiting to reestablish itself. How? Lots of activities can spark our mindfulness—whatever gives us periods of space and peace and solitude or takes us from distraction into fully focusing on what we're doing: Taking a moment to pause, notice, and reflect rather than barging ahead. Listening instead of speaking. Contemplative prayer. Spending time in our garden. Doing yoga or martial arts. Swimming some laps. Pausing for a shared family moment of silence before we start our meal.

There are also formal practices that cultivate mindfulness deeply. For me, it was the practice of sitting silently and paying attention to my breath that I first learned many years ago. For my grandparents, it was devoutly praying the rosary. For one of my favorite priests growing up, Father Crumbley, it was about centering prayer, a form of Christian meditation. Mindfulness itself is not a religion. Practicing it does not require giving up religious faith, or adopting a "foreign" faith, or becoming religious if you are not so inclined. But if you already embrace a religious practice, mindfulness can support you in deepening it. Being mindful can also help you actually be present in your house of worship when you are there. It will help you actually *be* there with attention when you are praying or telling your prayer beads. It will help you listen more closely to the sermon and be more deeply involved in the ritual. While meditation is often thought of as something strictly belonging to Eastern religion, in fact, various forms of meditation (which I think enable people to become mindful) have existed in religious communities since ancient times. According to the 2014 Religious Landscape Study from the Pew Research Center, "many Christians, including

49% of evangelical Protestants, 40% of Catholics and 55% of members of the historically black Protestant tradition also say they meditate once a week or more." (See Appendix A: Religious and Spiritual Mindful Practices for information about mindfulness practices in various traditions.)

While each of us may find different practices and habits to cultivate our mindfulness, the result will be the same: more peace of mind and a more consistent awareness of what really matters in life. I have conviction about mindfulness because I have experienced its power in my own life in these past few years, by means of the formal mindfulness practice I've received training in. I started practicing yoga back in college to deal with multiple football injuries, and I have a regular yoga practice now as a result. When I first practiced yoga, I was drawn to the periods of silent, motionless practice at the end of class, but those sessions are very brief. My first in-depth experience of mindfulness was on a five-day silent retreat with Jon Kabat-Zinn, two days after the 2008 presidential election. I left my two BlackBerries at the door and took the opportunity to call a time-out and take stock. By slowing my mind down, I could see the *root* of some of my troubles, not just the troubles themselves. I could see how stories I conjured in my head created unrealistic expectations that led to stress: I ought to be doing this, I ought to be doing that, I ought to be someone other than who I am. I could see how the stress increased and began to rule the roost.

I wish someone had taught me this skill when I was a kid. How many troubles I could have avoided!

I entered politics as a young man to do what so many of us would like to do: change the world. Over time, with the help of many mentors and some early stabs at mindfulness practice, I realized that if I wanted to change the world, I needed to first change myself. I also began to feel that if we as a society want to change the world, we need to tap into this amazing gift we've been given. I knew that Phil Jackson, the winningest coach in NBA history, had used mindfulness practices with his players to clear their minds and increase their performance. I was also encouraged to find out that mindfulness was already being taught to thousands of patients in hundreds of hospitals, to students and teachers in many schools across the nation, in our military, and in innovative programs in our inner cities. But it is far from enough. It's only a beginning. Cultivating our natural mindfulness needs to become a normal part of American life.

Wouldn't you give this practice a try if you knew it could help quiet your mind or increase your ability to focus, whether at work or on the golf course, tennis court, or yoga mat? You might notice your body being a little more relaxed and less tense, which would help you navigate the day with more ease. You might notice that you have a little more energy because you have less mental chatter and physical anxiety. You might find that you can fall asleep quicker and get a better night's rest. You might find yourself paying a little closer attention when your spouse or coworker is talking to you. Mindfulness is not a magic bullet or cure-all, but it can lead to small but significant changes that can improve your performance and make life more enjoyable. For example, one study, by Sara Lazar of Harvard University's Massachusetts General Hospital, showed cognitive and psychological benefits for participants in an eight-week mindfulness practice program. Other studies have shown greater feelings of well-being, increased attention span, and enhanced resilience after mindfulness programs. We'll consider these studies beginning in Chapter 3.

If these benefits are to spread beyond our personal lives, we need to support exciting, innovative programs like the ones I will talk about in this book—bringing a variety of forms of mindfulness into schools, hospitals, juvenile detention halls, and military bases, to name a few. And these programs are not for an elite few members of the Me Generation. One educator I know told me about a program she was doing for teachers in a small rural high school where a football coach couldn't say enough about how it not only made his students listen to him more often but actually heightened their performance and self-confidence—and made them kinder. She said tears were about to fall on his NRA T-shirt.

We Americans will always have our political differences, but mindfulness is something we can all share that transcends our differences and helps us negotiate them. The evidence I've seen tells me that as we bring mindfulness into health care, we will find a tool that helps us take care of ourselves better and see the roots of many of our problems. An increase in self-care not only makes us feel better but it also costs our system less, allowing us to focus more of our resources on illnesses beyond our control. When we bring mindfulness into education, we help our students increase their attention, decrease their stress, and work more creatively with their social emotions. And teachers find they pay better attention to the real needs of all their students and foster a better classroom atmosphere. When we bring mindfulness into the military, we help to enhance the greatest resource we have to ensure our own security and defense, something more powerful than any high-tech weaponry: well-functioning, high-performing *human beings* who have refined situational awareness. When we bring mindfulness into our approaches to energy, the environment, and the economy, we can find ways to live more simply while discovering a kind of prosperity that doesn't abuse our planet. When the caregivers and social workers who aid the most troubled people in our society bring mindfulness into the street, you would be surprised by how they can help the most traumatized people find courage and heart—and how the practice can help the caregivers prevent in themselves the burnout that plagues their professions.

What would an *education system* look like if each teacher approached each student with awareness of not only their own fears, worries, and concerns but also those of their students? How much better could students do if, instead of worrying about what others thought of them, they mobilized their attention and could bring more relaxation and focus to the task at hand?

Imagine what our *health-care system* would look like, and how we could lower the cost of becoming well, if more people became aware of their own conditions earlier and therefore participated more in preventing disease. Imagine what our *energy policy* would look like if every citizen became more aware of their own impact on the planet. Imagine what our *economy* would look like if our citizens had more faith in their ability to educate themselves on a lifelong basis, approaching getting an advanced degree or new training with eagerness rather than dread. Imagine how many problems we could solve if we tapped into the natural creativity we have inside us.

My job as a political leader, and the reason I am writing this book, is to find ways to help us solve our problems—as individual citizens and together as a nation. Mindfulness is not only a practice; it's a fundamental human capacity, and it can be accessed in many ways other than the classic mindfulness practice that I do. I believe firmly, though, that to solve the daunting problems I've talked about here, we need to apply some mindfulness.

In this book I will introduce you to people who are already benefitting from mindfulness and who are bringing it into the areas of society I have been talking about. You can get a glimpse of real positive change that is taking place and that could take place on a larger scale. And you may be moved to look into whether it makes sense to bring mindfulness to your own life and your own community.

If we shift our perspective through even a small amount of awareness, it can bring about enormous changes.

What You Can Do

One of the first things you can do is ask yourself, and maybe your friends and loved ones, some important basic questions:

- Am I stressed out? Is it affecting how I get along with my loved ones and perform at my job? Does it seem that stress is affecting our whole country? Where can we see this stress playing out in our national life?

- Am I paying attention to what is truly important to me in life? Are we as Americans paying attention to the truly important things in our national life?

- Am I in touch with the values in my heart that make it worth getting up in the morning? Are we as a nation in touch with the fundamental values that make us feel united as a people and determined to make our country stronger?

- Could I be helped by regular sessions of quiet, still, reflective, focused time? Could it help our leaders? Could it help our nation?

- When do I find time for moments of quiet and reflection? Can I find them more often?

CHAPTER 2

DISCOVERING MINDFULNESS

*I went to the woods because I wished
to live deliberately, to front only the essential
facts of life, and see if I could not learn what
it had to teach, and not, when I came to die,
discover that I had not lived.*

— HENRY DAVID THOREAU

It was cold and gray outside as I walked by the bottom of an imposing mountain. It felt as though fall had turned into winter in just a few hours. Snow was falling on my face as I walked—silently and slowly—beneath still-colorful trees. Leaves crackled under my weight as my foot hit the ground. I heard water moving over rocks in the small stream just a few feet to my left. In that moment, I was completely awake to life. My body relaxed, my brow unfurled. Something just happened, but I wasn't doing anything. I just let it be. The landscape looked crisper; my breath in the cold air entranced me. It felt as if a cloud had lifted from my eyes. I had no desire to be elsewhere— no thoughts about a better place. There was nothing to achieve or anything to prove to anyone else. I didn't have to defend a political position and felt no need to prove my self-worth through running for office. I didn't need to win an argument or drive a point home. I didn't need to be liked. I didn't crave affirmation. I was . . . okay. I literally just *was*.

In so many ways, the depth of mindfulness I was now experiencing contradicted my worldview, my belief in the need to be the one to "make it happen." But the feeling I experienced was not forced. Rather, I seemed to have allowed it to happen.

As I continued walking, that blissful moment of awareness slipped away. I realized, though, that I had tasted something I'd never experienced before. That fleeting moment left me with a level of clarity I'd never known. The clarity was not something created as much as discovered; something that had been there all along. I began to see my thoughts and examine them with an awareness similar to—but not quite as profound as—the awareness that had just dissipated.

They began coming up rapid fire:

Where did that feeling go?
How do I get it back?
Why was it so elusive?
What did I do wrong?

I started to turn on myself. *How did I mess things up? I'll never be mindful. What am I doing here on this retreat anyway? I should be working.*

My body began to tighten, my forehead wrinkled, and my mind was running like a wild horse. *There are hundreds of events I could be at if I were home where I should be. If I don't get home, I'll probably lose thousands of votes and maybe my next election. If I lose my election, my political career is dead. Will I ever reach my full potential? Will I live up to the expectations of my family and friends?* And so on. The inner voice was shrill and harsh.

Holy shit! I thought. *What just happened? How did things take such a quick turn for the worse?*

Fortunately, after days of practice and instruction at a Power of Mindfulness retreat led by Jon Kabat-Zinn at the Menla Mountain Retreat Center in upstate New York in November 2008, the training had taken root. The runaway horses of my mind were pulled to a halt, and I just breathed in and out.

⌒

The retreat began with all of us—busy people with hectic lives and lots of responsibilities—trying to get in touch with what was happening in our bodies at any given moment and how our thoughts have a direct effect on them. For example, we were each given a raisin to look at, examine, and put up to (but not in) our mouths. Have you ever just looked at one raisin? I'm normally inclined to rip open a box and dump them in my mouth. Here, we had to gaze at them, and as I put the raisin close to my lips, my mouth began to water. The raisin was not *in* my mouth, yet my body was preparing for it. The point was that what we see, hear, and think about in our mind has a direct effect on our bodies.

After becoming aware of the body-mind connection, we began over the course of five days to gradually reduce how much we talked. We observed extended periods of silence during which Jon guided us in mindfulness meditation. Some of us sat in chairs and some on cushions with our legs crossed. We followed our breath, in and out, in and out, for 30 or 45 minutes at a time. We spent an equal amount of time in walking meditation, inside or outside. I always chose outside, regardless of the weather. It was just so pleasurable to be out in the elements, appreciating nature without taking out my BlackBerry and snapping a picture. During walking meditation, we walked very slowly and deliberately, focusing on all of the movements our bodies made as we walked: the foot slowly lifting up, the knee pulling the lower part of the leg, the foot gently hitting the ground, heel first, then the middle of the foot, then the toes, becoming more grounded in the body. The process is very much like the attention that a long-distance runner or cyclist needs to bring to all of the body's systems—to have an overall awareness of how things are going.

Whether walking or sitting, though, my mind would wander off to family or work. Highly charged emotional thoughts would sometimes take me for a ride for an entire 30-minute session. I would open my eyes afterward and think to myself, *I just spent a half hour somewhere other than right here!* At times, it seemed so absurd I had to just laugh at myself.

We were taught to become aware of when our mind was wandering . . . and then, without judgment, to gently place our attention back on our breath or our bodies. It seems simple enough, but many times the wandering mind wins the day. You find yourself having conversations with people who are not even in the room; you're having heated arguments with people 400 miles away. I was not actually arguing with anyone, but I was making a story up in my head that took my body and psyche on a fantastical emotional roller coaster.

Have you ever woken up thinking about someone you're going to deal with that day and set off a chain reaction of thoughts about past encounters, slights, and irritations? By the time you see them that day, you are not meeting them with an open mind. Your thinking is predetermining the outcome. And before you know it, you're arguing. A little bit of awareness, I was discovering, helps us see that process and understand that we have a choice. We can respond with conscious choices to life's challenges, rather than simply react and overreact on the basis of habitual (and often negative) thought patterns.

Many of the thoughts and arguments cooked up in my head were advanced to protect the idea of who I thought I was. My idea of self, my ego, has this story of who I should be: congressman, rising star in politics, former quarterback, everybody likes me, smart . . . all these things. If I had a negative thought that threatened this story, like when someone once told me I was stupid, I would confront the thought and argue the ego's side of the story: "I am smart and here are three thousand reasons why. . . . Take that!" I felt a lot of tension rise in my body in response to this torrent of thoughts.

Throughout the retreat, we were reminded to come back to our breath and surf on it without working too hard to pay attention to it. Jon gently suggested that we might begin to notice how tiring it is to keep up our big-deal story. As the week moved on, we spent an entire 36 hours in silence. (Imagine that on Capitol Hill!) As we reached the heart of the retreat, it became clear how much time and energy we all waste in our inner World War over nothing. We fight and defend and argue—all in an imaginary world in our heads. And then we wonder why we can't sleep at night or we have high blood pressure or anxiety or are cranked up on stress hormones. The deeper the silence became, the deeper I realized the inanity, even the insanity, of putting so much effort into fictional story lines rather than listening to and noticing what's happening in and around me at any given moment.

Many times we turn on ourselves for having "bad thoughts." Mindfulness teaches that this is just how our mind works. It is the nature of the mind to generate thoughts. No need to beat ourselves up over it. Be kind to yourself. Don't judge. Let it go. This doesn't mean we shouldn't use our brains to evaluate and analyze thoughts and issues. There is a time and place to use the analyzing brain. But the brain works for us; we do not work for it. Our brain is here to serve our hearts, not the other way around.

Our society suffers, I think, from an overemphasis on the intellect and an aversion to matters of the heart— as if they were somehow un-American. Jon used poems and stories to illustrate the potency of the heart. The less chitchat that was in my brain, the more the poems touched me. Having my heart opened up like that reminded me of my oldest nephew, Nicolas. He's five and attends a Catholic preschool with the Oblate Sisters in Youngstown. After school one day, Nicky's teacher told his mother that at the end of every school day, she plays classical music as they all clean the classroom. And every day, Nicolas cries when he hears it. Sister says that it "just touches him so much." How beautiful! How do we as a society teach our kids, our parents, everyone, to maintain that connection to the miracles all around us? Perfectly composed music or art, the wonders of nature, even our own ability to breathe—all are miracles. To feel that, we have to stop living only in our heads and also live in our hearts.

Some of the poems Jon read were from American giants like Thoreau or Emerson. I started to see mindfulness as very much in line with the values of America. Our founding fathers acted from the heart when they transformed our world by stating that "all men are created equal," "endowed by their Creator with certain unalienable rights" such as life, liberty, and happiness.

It seems to me it would do us all good to act from our hearts more often. We would be surprised how small acts of attention and kindness can release the energy, enthusiasm, and imagination bottled up in our overstressed minds and bodies. We have tried a million times to *think* our way to a better society. But our thinking doesn't work so well if it's not aligned with what we feel deep in our hearts, our inspirations and aspirations, our innermost desire. We need to realign ourselves the way a GPS in a car recalibrates the route. When our wandering mind takes us away from our heart, we need to pause and realign ourselves with the values we have stored there. We can then remember what motivates and inspires us to get up and take on the challenges of each day. I learned that for myself up on the mountain.

⌒

Of course, eventually you have to come off the mountain and reenter the everyday world. I knew things would not be as peaceful when I returned to Capitol Hill, but I felt as if I'd received some training that would help me meet the challenges of life with more eagerness and skill. On the walk in the woods I described earlier, it was gratifying to see how the training enabled me to separate from the nattering voice in my head and return to the breath. When the thoughts took me over, they were confining. The more I noticed the breath and focused on the rhythm of walking, the more the sensation of spaciousness returned. When the thoughts started to creep back into my awareness, I saw them differently. Most important, I *saw* them.

The thoughts continued to be judgmental and critical. In fact, they were mean. It became apparent to me
that such thoughts tend to recur. They can be like back-
ground noise. I had just never noticed them. As they
revealed themselves to me, I realized I could be terribly
hard on myself. I could judge myself with a level of cru-
elty I wouldn't inflict on my worst enemy. I could get
stuck in a thought loop of questioning past decisions or
regretting remarks I made or lines in speeches I'd given.
It was repeated pressure, always self-imposed. I thought
I was kind, compassionate, and considerate. It turns
out that was true only if I was dealing with someone
other than myself. But toward myself I could be cruel,
unforgiving, dissatisfied, manipulative, mean-spirited,
and needlessly judgmental. I started to think about my
new nephew and how I would never treat him this way.
Toward everyone else I was the town nice guy; toward
myself I was the town asshole.

It turns out that over the years, I had unknowingly
created a big story in my head. I shared it with no one, not
even my own conscious mind. I needed to have a highly
successful political career, marry the perfect woman, be
worth millions of dollars, and write a few books and movies. And if I didn't do all of this, my family and friends
would see me as an underachiever. How tiring! I couldn't
believe I had spent so much time and energy trying to
uphold a story I created in my own head.

I was so caught up in my story that I missed my
life. All of the accomplishments: one of the youngest
state senators in Ohio history, a member of the United
States Congress at 29 years old, world traveler, someone
who met Presidents and prime ministers. But I was not
entirely there for all of those events because more than a
few times, I was somewhere else in my mind. Fortunately,

not every moment of my life was lived unaware. There were times when, whether through adrenaline or grace, I was focused and aware, in the zone. But I was absent for plenty of other moments because I was always trying to fit the moment into the context of the story I had created in my mind. How was my life playing in Peoria?

Watching this crazy story line from a distance, I decompressed. The pain, the hurt, the judgments dropped away. And then I was in a state of disbelief that I had missed so much of my life. But now I could breathe. The pressure evaporated. The mindfulness retreat at the foot of the Catskills rocked my world. And now I felt that I wanted to share what I had experienced with my family and friends. I wanted to teach it to my two-year-old nephew, to my brother, to my mom. "Everybody get off the roller coaster—I've found the answer!" I wanted to scream out. Okay, so I was getting a little carried away. Maybe this wasn't for everybody, but nonetheless I was intrigued. This seems so simple, and it works. Why didn't anyone teach me this when I was a kid? Why are we not teaching this in schools? Students could learn so much more effectively if their heads were clearer. Why is this not a part of our health-care system? The stress that causes so many diseases could be greatly diminished and save our society billions of dollars. Everyone in our country is on the treadmill. Scrambling, working, pulled in a million different directions. Mindfulness won't eliminate the responsibilities and pressures that cause us to become so scattered, but it can arm us with a way of being that allows us to deal with them more effectively. We teach most people to drive, and cultivating mindfulness is a skill more basic than that. Why don't we teach it to a whole lot more people?

At that moment, I decided I would advocate in Congress and on the Appropriations Committee for integrating mindfulness into key aspects of our society. Because the committee I was sitting on funds health care, research, and education, I could use my position to help mindfulness become an element of various government programs. I had tried to use my life and talents to relieve people's suffering through social and economic justice. But I realized at the retreat in the Catskills that if I truly wanted to relieve people's suffering and make modest attempts to improve the social and economic situation of our country, there was more I could do. As I saw it, there would be no better way to help people than to dedicate my work to integrating mindfulness into health care, education, and society at large. If we could teach our citizens how to take better care of themselves by working with their minds—the source of so much stress, pain, and difficulty—we would prevent manifold problems and save a great deal of money.

Taking responsibility is a core American value, going back to the founding of this country. I had read shelf-loads of history books, studied constitutional law, and been a legislator for 10 years, but I never understood life, liberty, and the pursuit of happiness so intimately as I did during that retreat in November 2008. As the retreat ended and the time was coming to head back into political life, I set out to better understand my own life and my own capacity for noticing destructive thoughts, emotions, story lines, and habit patterns and learn to loosen the grip they can have on me. I undertook this journey knowing that happiness cannot be pursued. It can only be revealed. I resolved that my life would no longer be driven by doing one thing after another or getting ahead or getting a new title. It would be guided more by seeing the wonder that unfolds in daily life and the millions of miracles that happen moment to moment. And it would be guided by noticing and letting go of undue stress that hampered my performance and limited the attention I could pay to my work and to the needs of others. Without preaching or proselytizing, I wanted to share what one teacher has called "the miracle of mindfulness" with my friends, family, and fellow citizens—and seek to discover the ways in which we already live mindfully and express it through our actions.

My best friend, Billy Leonard, and I were inseparable throughout the first 13 years of our lives. It seemed like we laughed like fools our entire adolescence, the kind of joyful, deep belly laughs that only kids have. We were both younger brothers, born three weeks apart. Our older brothers—Rick Leonard, who now runs all my offices in Ohio, and my brother Al, who has run all my campaigns—were driven nuts by our antics. And our parents would sometimes laugh just because we were laughing. We did everything together and seemed to find the humor in just about any situation. We laughed so hard sometimes it would make us cry. In recent memory, the only time I have heard a laugh like that is when I've been around the Dalai Lama. I have met the Dalai Lama on several occasions. Inevitably, at some point during his talk or conversation, he would let out a deep, childlike belly laugh. There's an infectious, immediate goodness to it. Each time I've reflected on his laughing that way, I've wondered why I don't laugh like that much anymore. Life loads us up with so much baggage that we forget how to experience simple joy like Billy and I did when we were young. We constantly focus on our fears, inadequacies, and to-do lists. And the anxiety and fear paralyze us. They reduce our awareness and cut off the spontaneity needed to be surprised by a well-timed joke or life's irony.

This habit of ruminating on our weaknesses makes life less rich. It's not much fun. Besides, isn't the goal in life to be cheerful rather than in a constant state of worry? Isn't our world meant to be enjoyed and bathed in, not rejected as a scary place? We catch glimpses of joy on vacation or when certain moments of instant rapture grab us and arrest our worrying. Our child's first steps, a baby's smile, a success at work or school, a sublime music performance, feeling connected to others as we cheer together at a sporting event or sing along at a rock concert, a deep gaze into our lover's eyes, or making love with true intimacy—these special moments are too few. But they are so emotionally powerful they break through our habits and ruminations.

All too soon after such moments, it seems, we quickly cut off this life force by returning to our well-practiced habits of worry and concern. But I learned that if I pay close attention to the sensations in my body and the thoughts in my head—if I experience the moment with *mindfulness*—I can catch these habits as they begin to lead me back down the same old path. With enough practice we can override this behavior with an intention to be more alive for more of those beautiful moments.

When aren't miracles happening? Just consider how many life processes are going on in your body right this second. Thousands. Consider everything going on in the world around you in just this moment. It's magical, if you really look at it. But we miss the deeper dimensions of what's going on because we are focused on what went bad in the past and what we anticipate will go wrong in the future. That rare moment when we rediscover that childlike magic is familiar to us all. It's what Dave Matthews is talking about in his song "Old Dirt Hill," when he sings, "Bring that beat back to me again." We long for that childlike ease and joy.

Once, when I was part of a congressional delegation to Pakistan and India, we visited a heartbreakingly poor Indian village, so undeveloped that the sewer and well water ran together. During a lighter moment of the trip, we were in the audience for a traditional song and dance performance when I found myself surrounded by a throng of giggling children. The kids were terrific—smiling, laughing, goofing around, just like Billy and I would have been doing, including getting scolded for misbehaving, like kids everywhere. They didn't know how poor they were. They were joyfully alive and in the moment.

Mindfulness practice can train us to be like that—to free ourselves from mental burdens that we create out of our tendency to treat our worries as solid, permanent realities. We can see how when we solidify our thoughts, it steals our ability to be alive in the precious few moments we have on this planet. How many times have we worried like hell about something and later found out that there really was nothing to worry about? This type of worrying wastes our time and also has a negative physiological effect on our bodies. It increases our stress levels, which in turn release hormones to deal with the stress. Long and protracted levels of stress and the subsequent hormone-release damage our bodies and, literally, take years off our lives. Days, months, and sometimes years of *dis*ease in our minds result in many forms of disease in our bodies.

Of course, adulthood presents us with challenges and crises that we all must face directly. I would never try to diminish the severity or pain of job loss, grave illness, or the loss of loved ones. We all experience serious sources of stress on a regular basis. I know I do, along with my family and my many constituents. But take a moment to consider what serves us best in dealing with the highs and lows in life.

Lately, I've had more opportunity to notice and reflect on what passes me by when I'm not present, when I'm existing "a short distance from [my] body," as James Joyce says of his character Mr. Duffy. I'm starting to catch myself when I'm with my nephews and nieces, so that instead of drifting off into thinking about legislative priorities, I stay with the children. I feel a connection to them even when words are not spoken. In work-related conversations, I find myself letting the distractions go more often than I used to and really listening to my colleagues and co-workers. When my constituents grab me at events, I'm more frequently present to listen to their whole story, not just pigeonhole it. Many stories are heart-wrenching, and some are beautiful. But I try my best to be there for them and not mentally move on to my next meeting or appointment. This is no special talent. It's just developing the ability we all have for peacefulness and attention, the same kind my grandfather exhibited when he spent time with us. His caring was all the more powerful because it was calm and focused.

✑

Because of the times we live in, it can be hard to appreciate the joy and simplicity that await us in the present moment. Our media outlets bombard us with horror and war and death and disease 24/7. Yes, to be good citizens we need to be informed, but do we need to be scared out of our wits? Do we need to depress ourselves with a steady diet of cynicism and negativity? For life to be in balance, we need to find moments of peace and inner strength, what the mythologist Joseph Campbell talked about as sacred places and ministers call sanctuary. We need deep inner resources to take on the big personal and societal challenges we face. Can we be a force for change by personally committing to being present and alive in each moment and deriving our enjoyment out of that? And if pain and suffering come our way, can we be present for them too, as opposed to just watching them on television? And can we be present for others as they are suffering?

I find that people I'm talking to these days are tired of the fear-based world—the world we want to hide from by balling ourselves up into a cocoon. I believe people want to return to the free and easy feeling of the childhood we once had—or wished we did—because it includes joy and laughter. We want to bring that beat back again. We need to find a way to do it, for ourselves and for our communities.[2]

During the early years of my political career, I had very little campaign money. One way to combat that problem was by going to where the largest number of people would show up every day. We acquired an Ohio Department of Transportation map that showed the busiest intersections in my district. Every morning and afternoon rush hour, in the rain, snow, sleet, or hail, we were there holding signs. People appreciated our daily effort, and many said that if I was willing to work that hard to get the job, they felt they could trust me to work that hard for them once I had it.

Standing there watching folks, we could learn a lot from their faces. It was amazing to see how many people were preoccupied and worried as they went to work. And there was a huge difference in people's attitude on Monday morning as compared to Friday afternoon. During the week, many people looked unhappy. I used to make it a point to try to make them smile by waving and smiling. Sometimes it worked, and sometimes it pissed them off even more and they would flip me the middle finger. But on Fridays it was much different. Music was on and people were flashing smiles. Some were stopping to pick up a few beers. It seemed that for those couple of weekend days, they were getting their lives back.

Is this really our lot? Does happiness come only on the weekend? Can we find a way to be more cheerful every day of the week?

As I've pointed out, we have lots of problems in our country. But I've come to believe that a key element in taking on those challenges effectively is our own inner strength, resiliency, and awareness of who we really are. We need to believe we have the capacity to transform our own lives, to innovate with our own mind and body. And that transformation will change the world. Maybe not in a monumental way at first, but if we're patient, changes will occur. A building is constructed one brick at a time.

I admit that I can bug people sometimes with my rampant enthusiasm. It's not always infectious. But I'm also realistic, and at times wary. I've been burned many times by accepting things on faith alone or trying to convince everyone that my experience could be replicated for them. I knew that for mindfulness to come into public life with government support, it would have to be based on scientific evidence. I decided to visit researchers to find out why and how mindfulness works—and above all why it is relevant to our daily lives and to our society's key institutions.

My own experience took me most of the way to believing in the power of mindfulness to effect change, but what the researchers showed me sealed the deal. When I heard what they had to say—which I recount in the next chapter—it reminded me of a story Joseph Campbell used to tell about overhearing two children talking about evolution:

First child: Well, how do they know that it's true?
Second child: They found the bones!

WHAT YOU CAN DO

- Interested in trying out mindfulness practice? See if anybody in your city or town is teaching mindfulness. Check with a Y, church, synagogue, or yoga center. Do they have a mindfulness class? Try Googling *mindfulness* in your area and see what results come up.

- Consider taking a few minutes of quiet every day, when you can. Just start where you are, perhaps when you're about to begin work at your desk or in the break area, right before an evening meal, or after you put your children to bed.

- Download an app for your phone or a program for your computer that rings a bell periodically as a reminder to reconnect with the present moment.

- If you're lucky enough to have the time, one of the best ways to dive into mindfulness is to take a few days away from the hectic pace of your life and find some quiet time—with the help of any form of qualified instruction in paying attention to your mind without judgment.

- Find a place that offers silent retreats for as little as one day or a weekend, or even longer if you like. There are many different kinds of retreats, so do some searching and find one that you think might suit you and your circumstances.

CHAPTER 3

WHAT SCIENTISTS SAY MINDFULNESS CAN DO FOR YOU

If we provide concrete evidence of the benefits of mindfulness practice, more people will at least try it and see if it is beneficial for them.

— SARA LAZAR

Our alarm goes off on a cold, dark morning. For some of us it is an obnoxious buzzing that startles us from our sleep and we jump out of bed. Our first experience of the new day is agitation. Or it may be a cool sound emanating from our smartphone. It may be an easier wake-up call than the traditional blaring of the old alarm clock, but it usually brings us into immediate contact with the cyber world. We hit the snooze or dismiss the alarm only to see that someone texted or e-mailed us since we fell asleep. We read the message and our mind races to solve the problem at work or address the conflict in a personal relationship. We may or may not reply, but our brain and heart are already feeling the stress.

We carry that stress with us downstairs as we begin to make our morning coffee. We put the television on to see and hear what is going on in the world. (Just to make sure we are all still alive.) More often than not the news is pretty bad: a couple of murders happened yesterday, a terrorist plot to blow up planes in Europe, an earthquake in Pakistan, a possible hurricane will hit somewhere in Florida or the Gulf Coast, the U.S. is going bankrupt, people on Wall Street got caught cheating again, and pensions on Main Street will be diminished.

We drink our coffee as we flip through the newspaper in print or online. More bad news, with a laundry list of local problems like school levies not passing, libraries closing, and a local factory shutting down. We have barely finished our first cup and we have been inundated with negative information. We are off on the wrong foot. We have been ripped out of the present moment and are thinking about something that is not happening directly to us or in need of immediate attention in that moment. Before long, we're driving our child to school and ignoring her because in our mind we're worried that she might do poorly on a test or get hurt during phys ed. Most of us get thrown out of balance because we are not physically or mentally equipped to handle all of the negativity happening around the world 24 hours a day. We are not wired to deal with a bombardment of perceived stressors on a consistent basis. It's like putting a V-8 engine into a Volkswagen Beetle. At some point the body of the car can't keep up and is literally out of control.

As stress harms our body and mind and makes us less effective in dealing with the challenges of our daily lives, so too does it spread harm throughout our society. If an epidemic of a debilitating disease were spreading in schools, hospitals, social service agencies, and the military, we would declare a national emergency, and the Centers for Disease Control would be taking energetic steps to do something about it. In fact, high levels of stress are affecting all of our institutions and we need to do something about it.

Our species is more inclined to pay attention to negative information than to great news. After all, we need to be aware of what might harm us. As the neuropsychologist Dr. Rick Hanson, founder of the Wellspring Institute for Neuroscience and Contemplative Wisdom and author of *Hardwiring Happiness: The New Brain Science of Contentment, Calm, and Confidence*, put it to me, our ancestors stayed alive to pass on their genes by continually looking for threats and then revving up with stress hormones to fight or flee. These intense reactions to life-threatening situations helped us live to develop increasingly creative survival mechanisms: tools and weapons, beautiful languages to further our ability to survive, and eventually the industrial world and modern science and technology.

If we are not aware of its power, though, our own survival instinct and the mechanisms it sets in motion could quickly turn us into an endangered species. Our survival mechanism causes us to fear what we don't understand. It rears its ugly head in our person-to-person dealings with life's challenges. On a collective level, we can be gripped by fear that spreads like a virus in the body politic and affects our group decision-making. In modern times, collective fear has emboldened demagogues and fearmongers the world over. It has led to unnecessary wars and senseless ethnic cleansing.

Our country has also made reckless and mindless decisions because our survival instinct has evolved—or devolved, as some may think—into trying to make as much money as we can, sometimes sacrificing all other values. This thinking led us to the conclusion, either consciously or subconsciously, that we literally could not survive as a country unless we went to war for oil or propped up a dictator in a failed state we had "interests" in. Being mindful means being aware of both our individual and collective stress and the consequences it can bring. Stress can save our lives, but it can also kill us.

⌒

Mindfulness helped me become aware of how my body and mind reacted to the stress of daily life, to get in touch with how my built-in survival mechanism could go into high gear when it had no valid reason to. I could feel myself tense up when someone told me something I didn't want to hear. I would lose focus during a conversation because I was fretting about something that happened hours before. I would look at my BlackBerry messages first thing in the morning and get thrown into a tailspin before I even got out of bed. This made me curious as to what exactly is happening to the brain and nervous system when we are constantly taking in all of this negativity and whether mindfulness could help with it.

To begin to explore questions about stress and mindfulness, I paid a visit to Jon Kabat-Zinn and his wife, Myla, shortly after the Catskills retreat. Jon and many of his fellow scientific researchers had similar questions about mindfulness, stress, and negativity. How does being mentally *out of* the "present moment" influence our physical and mental health? How does being *in* the present moment affect our brains and bodies? How do stressful situations impact our brains and nervous systems? How do *constant* states of stress affect our well-being? The only difference between my questions and theirs is that they started asking these questions 30 years ago. They are true pioneers in the field of mind/body research. And over the past decade or so, the body of research in this field has grown exponentially. We now know we have more control over our health and well-being than we ever thought possible.

Practices that cultivate mindfulness give us a real-world approach to dealing with stress. Jon explained that stress is dealt with in the two parts of our autonomic nervous system, along with various regions of the brain. Our innate stress response ramps up our *sympathetic* nervous system, which primes us for our fight-or-flight-or-freeze response—fight it out with the predator, get out of there fast, or freeze in a state of indecision between the two. Our *parasympathetic* nervous system, fortunately, can counteract the effects of the sympathetic nervous system and help establish a calm yet alert state.

Practicing mindfulness brings our body, Jon told me, into a "real dynamic equilibrium, a genuine resting state. In that state, we are not only both alert and direct, but also very open. It quiets the sympathetic nervous system." Mindfulness brings our body into balance by quieting down the very part of our nervous system that gets all whacked out when we are stressed out and by reinforcing a sense of alert calmness. If we just stop for a few minutes a day and gently bring attention to our breath or our body, we can slow down the stress response. We can gain control of our own bodies and therefore reduce our stress and anxiety. Reducing stress allows our bodies and minds to work at an optimal level and use our energy more efficiently—and that in turn affects how we breathe, how we eat, and how we sleep. Just as the effects of our stress response spread rapidly throughout the body, making us feel tense or exhausted, so too do the effects of mindfulness spread throughout the various systems, improving the way we carry ourselves throughout our day.

A significant benefit of mindfulness is that with less stress, it seems that our body can heal itself more quickly. Jon and his colleagues conducted a study on patients with psoriasis. This skin disease is traditionally treated by putting patients in a light box for brief exposures to ultraviolet light over a period of months to try to heal the skin. The study involved having patients practice mindfulness while in the light box. The results were astonishing. In the meditating group, the skin healed four times faster than in the control group. These patients required fewer treatments than the nonmeditating group, suggesting that we could save thousands of dollars in health-care costs if the practice expanded to larger numbers of patients.

Studies like this suggest that if we reduce our stress and improve our well-being, we may reduce the severity of some conditions and even prevent certain conditions from emerging in the first place. For example, conditions that result from poor nutrition and poor attention to other aspects of health could be greatly ameliorated with mindfulness practice. Paying attention can help us counteract impulsive food buying and eating, and it can help us notice when we need to move around and exercise.

One of the most helpful research methods developed in the past few decades enables us to see what is going on in the brain via the fMRI. Most of us have heard of the MRI (magnetic resonance imaging), which helps detect tumors and other abnormalities. The fMRI, or "functional MRI," not only produces an image, but it produces a movie. And when you use an fMRI on the brain, you can watch brain function. It's one of the main tools that neuroscientist Dr. Richard Davidson's lab has used in studying the brains of mindfulness practitioners.

I traveled to the University of Wisconsin–Madison to visit with Dr. Davidson, whose impressive titles include William James and Vilas Research Professor of Psychology and Psychiatry, as well as director of the Waisman Laboratory for Brain Imaging and Behavior. He is also the co-author, together with Sharon Begley, of *The Emotional Life of Your Brain* and, most recently, of *Altered Traits: Science Reveals How Meditation Changes Your Mind, Brain, and Body* with Daniel Goleman. I was so excited to hear what he had to say that I flew up to Madison on Super Bowl Sunday. (That's quite a departure, given that I'm a former quarterback from Ohio's football belt.) We met for a long dinner and covered lots of terrain. I could not have been more impressed with his scope of knowledge and the calm and focused way he talked about it. His enthusiasm for the positive impact that mindfulness could have on society is contagious. But he's not an ideologue or a zealot; he is a scientist. He wants everything proven with hard-nosed research, and in particular neuroscience research. He is one of the most respected neuroscientists in the world, has received numerous grants from the National Institutes of Health, and founded the nationally renowned Center for Healthy Minds—where researchers are not only studying what can go wrong with our brains but are also trying to see how much our brains are truly capable of. If we can put a man on the moon, as the old saying goes, we can find new horizons for the capability of the human brain.

After dinner, we returned to Richie's home to join his wife and some friends in watching the second half of the Super Bowl. Early the next morning, a friend and colleague of mine from Wisconsin, then Congresswoman, now Senator Tammy Baldwin, met Richie at his office. Tammy is a wonderful, smart, and thoughtful progressive who is always looking for creative ways to improve our education and health-care systems. She too wanted to learn more about Richie's work. Neither of us was disappointed.

After giving us a brief tour of his cutting-edge lab, Richie explained some of the basics of the brain and how it works, because before we can cure our stress, he said, we need to be aware of what it really means at a physiological level. Our brain is only 2 percent of our body's mass but uses over 20 percent of its oxygen and glucose, substances needed to boost the brain's performance. Clearly, the brain is carrying a pretty heavy load. Given the complexities in American life today, the brain seems to be overworked and underpaid. Its responsibilities are vast and interconnected with every other part of our body. It's like a head nurse in an emergency room dealing rapidly with all the complexities of a medical crisis. It's the quarterback of our entire body: our nervous system, our hormone system, our organs. It takes in all of the external stimuli—threats, requests, demands, acts of kindness and love—and sends signals to other members on the team to respond to what the senses are picking up. Meanwhile, it also has to keep up basic maintenance of the body—breathing, digestion, blood flow, cell renewal, immune response, and other vital processes. In Richie's lab, you can see movies of the brain at work. It's a first-rate drama.

When a stressful situation comes upon us—a personal conflict with a co-worker, our daughter wanting to stay out after midnight, a road-rager disrupting the conference call we're conducting by Bluetooth while driving to work—the human mind and body handle it the same way they did 100,000 years ago. Two key parts of our brain are involved: the *hippocampus*, a small structure near the base of the brain with the size and shape of a small seahorse; and the *amygdala*, almond-shaped groups of nuclei in the midsection of the brain.

The perceptual information is arranged and passed to the hippocampus, which rapidly determines whether it's real or not. If the hippocampus identifies the incoming information as threatening, it sends alarm bells to the amygdala and we go into red alert, sending out the hormones that create the superfocus in our body and mind that put our ancestors in a position to deal with a wild animal on the attack.

Dr. Davidson reminded me that the stress-generating process has served our species well for thousands of years. We are here today because of it. As amazing and necessary as this process is, though, it is not meant to happen 24 hours a day, day in and day out. It's meant to happen only when our lives are at risk or when a major situation is at hand. One of the challenges for those of us alive today is that our brain and body cannot easily distinguish a real physical threat from an emotional one, like having a bad nightmare and waking up with a racing heart or recalling a traumatic event. The events in the nightmare didn't really happen; the traumatic event is not recurring.

Responding to perceived threats takes a toll on our bodies. The same goes for an anticipated negative future situation. Our body goes through the full-scale stress reaction. It's like bringing out all the fire engines and firefighters to a five-alarm fire that turns out to be a false alarm. If we live in a state of worry or regret, this process is going on inside of us all the time.

Should we really wonder why we are tired so often and why we can't seem to get our energy levels up? Why we drink too much or eat too much? All of the worry and negativity is setting our body off on a roller coaster of hormone release and decimating our nervous system. We get down, worn out, beat up. And when we get sick, Dr. Davidson says, all this stress makes it worse. "In cardiovascular disease or asthma, the evidence is incontrovertible that high levels of stress exacerbate these conditions," he told me. We ingest so much negativity that we make ourselves sick, and then the stress of the worry makes our health problem worse.

I went into a mild state of panic just hearing Richie say how we make things worse for ourselves. It makes you think about how often you're revving yourself up for no good reason. I remembered how often I worry about things that are out of my control. I thought of my mom, who worried her entire life about me and my brother . . . and still does. I remember how much my grandmother worried about us too. I guess that's where my mom learned it. But I always felt so bad about it because I never thought there was much achieved by it. Pray for us? Yes. Worry? That didn't make any sense.

I asked Richie what happens to our bodies when we are under stress for long periods of time. I was particularly interested because in my area of the country, so many people have lost good-paying jobs. I can feel the stress and heartache emanating from these friends and neighbors. I see 55-year-old people who have worked hard their whole lives lose everything. Mothers weep as they tell me about not having health care for their children. This is real-world stress that doesn't go away after a few minutes. It lasts for days, weeks, months, and years.

Whether someone has long periods of stress because of difficult, real-life challenges like job loss or lack of health care, or whether the stress is from self-created stories filled with negative thoughts that never come to pass, it leads to chronic stimulation of our sympathetic nervous system. Apparently, sustained stress causes inflammation in various parts of our body. We are literally inflamed, with all the negative effects that implies. This, then, leads to heart disease, depressed immune-system function (which leads to increased colds and flu), ulcers, type 2 diabetes, and even erectile dysfunction. Continuing stress also leads to decreased levels of serotonin, which leads to being in a bad mood much of the time. That's why when some of us come home, instead of having a convivial meal with our family—which studies have shown is highly beneficial for healthy relationships and child development—we poison the atmosphere with our blue funk.

If our amygdala is constantly ramped up, Richie told me, it eventually becomes ultrasensitive and leads to our wrongly viewing situations as threatening or dangerous. Like a trained muscle, the more the brain makes certain responses, the easier that response becomes. It's like a quarterback running a play so many times he can do it in his sleep. Our brain ends up making all the world look like a threatening place.

⌒

From talking to Jon and others, I also knew that mindfulness has a role to play in attention, focus, and peak performance, which are important for students, athletes, and critically, soldiers and others who respond to crises on our behalf. When psychologist Amishi Jha came to meet and talk with me in my congressional office in Washington, I began to learn more about these other dimensions of the power of mindfulness. I was reminded of the benefits that Bella seemed to be experiencing in her tae kwon do class and that I thought would be helpful for our schoolchildren and our teachers—and for our military. When I first met her, Dr. Jha was at the University of Pennsylvania. Now an associate professor within the department of psychology at the University of Miami, she heads the Jha Lab. With grants from the U.S. Department of Defense and several private foundations, her lab uses a variety of sophisticated monitoring techniques to investigate the promotion of resilience in people performing high-stress roles by using mind-training techniques that strengthen the brain's attention networks.

They're particularly interested in understanding how these systems work together to select and deselect information. They investigate how these processes of mental selection may be modified with training—including mindfulness-based training techniques. Dr. Jha led the research team in a study examining the effects of mindfulness training on soldiers during predeployment at Schofield Barracks in Hawaii. We'll discuss more about this project, which is the first of its kind to investigate the neural and behavioral consequences of resilience training for soldiers before they deploy in combat zones, in Chapter 6.

Amishi explained to me that "persistent and intensive demands, such as those experienced during high-stress intervals, may deplete our working memory capacity and lead to cognitive failures and emotional disturbances." An earlier study of Marines done by her team hypothesized that mindfulness training might be able to reduce these negative effects by bolstering working memory capacity. In that study, she told me, for those who practiced mindfulness diligently, working memory capacity increased. They also had lower levels of negative affect (emotion) and higher levels of positive affect—they were in a healthier frame of mind, poised for sounder decision making. These findings, she told me, suggest that "sufficient mindfulness practice may protect against impairments associated with high-stress contexts," such as those experienced by soldiers, firefighters, and nurses every day—and the rest of us at least some of the time.

In another study, Dr. Jha investigated the hypothesis that mindfulness training may alter or enhance specific aspects of attention. The results suggest that such training may help participants orient their attention and be more receptive and alert. Dr. Jha's studies, then, suggest that consistent practice of mindfulness actually increases our ability to mobilize our attention and direct it to one experience or another. Isn't this what our students need the most to excel in school, to do well in math and science, which is what every expensive national education initiative in the past several decades has insisted they must do?

Through enhancing focus, mindfulness could also be an important contributor to improving peak performance, which is vital not only for athletes but also for the many first responders we rely on to protect our well-being. We owe it to them, and to ourselves, to help them become the best they can be.

In thinking about the benefits of attention and focus, I was reminded that mindfulness itself requires attention and focus. As mindfulness increases our focus, it can increase our mindfulness in turn: a virtuous cycle, rather than the vicious cycle of repeated stress. But it does require us to commit to becoming at least a little bit more mindful and being mindful somewhat more consistently. Otherwise, mindfulness would just be a magic potion that required no work on our part.

Techniques that cultivate mindfulness are simple, but the persistent application is challenging. It takes discipline. I love what Katharine Hepburn once said: "Without discipline, there's no life at all." We needn't see discipline as impinging on the freedom we celebrate as Americans. In fact, it is quite the opposite, according to Jim Tressel, the highly successful head football coach of the Ohio State Buckeyes, in his book *The Winners Manual*:

> In today's culture, discipline is considered a negative, almost foul, word. We associate discipline with a strict, narrow lifestyle in which we're punished if we're not obedient. We tend to think that a disciplined life is restrictive and controlled by some outside authority figure with a sour disposition. In short, we think that a life of discipline means no freedom, no fun, and no joy. But nothing could be further from the truth. The fundamental of discipline will actually help us live more freeing, invigorating lives.

While discipline is often thought of as joyless, if we consider for a moment all the deep satisfaction often expressed by people who have engaged in a discipline for a long period of time, we can see discipline as an essential component of a meaningful life. We watch in wonder as marvelous actors, artists, athletes, and doctors practice their crafts. We honor them, spend lots of time enjoying their brilliance, and long to be like them in so many ways.

One attribute they all possess is discipline. In a mindful nation, discipline is delightful.

⌒

Meanwhile, what I learned about the effects of stress and inattention worried me. What if once we develop this stress superhighway, there is no turning back? There would be no light at the end of the tunnel of stress and mindless behavior. Neuroscientists have a rule of thumb, I was told: what fires together wires together. When neurons in our brain fire over and over again, they become hardwired to repeat the pattern. That's how we train ourselves to become great. It's also how our negative habit patterns become ingrained addictions we feel we can't shake.

Naturally, on this basis I assumed that repeated applications of our stress response would harden us and make it impossible to return our bodies and minds back to our pre-stress days. While growing up, we were told that if we wanted to learn a foreign language, we had to learn it when we were very young. Our brains would "harden" as we got older, and learning a foreign language at that point would be nearly impossible.

But the scientists presented me with good news: *neuroplasticity.*

The principle of neuroplasticity means that the brain can change and grow through our entire lifetime. This is one of the most encouraging discoveries in recent times, and it gives us all the more reason to want to practice mindfulness. "Neuroscientists discovered that everything they told us when I was a graduate student in biology about the nervous system was wrong," Jon told me, "in the sense that in certain regions of the nervous system you can make new functional neurons until the day you die. Particularly in the hippocampus, which is related to memory and learning. It turns out it's not all downhill from the time we're two years old." A smile came to my face as I realized that we have ongoing influence over how we are wired.

The fact that our brain is always changing means we're not "locked-in" to having the stress superhighway built into our nervous system. We can keep that road there for when we need it. The cutting-edge research today shows us how mindfulness can help us reshape our brain and nervous system. We mentioned how a lot of stress can hypercharge our amygdala, which in turn makes it thicker because of all the activity. Now studies by Dr. Sara Lazar suggest that after an eight-week mindfulness-based-stress-reduction (MBSR) program, at least one side of the amygdala gets thinner. By practicing mindfulness we can change the way our brain functions. Most important, we can change it in the direction of balance and, in fact, in the direction of kindness.

Mindfulness is also heartfulness, Jon told me during our talk. We can be calm, open, attentive, and gentle no matter how stressed out and self-absorbed we've become. We can transform worry into attention and caring. "We can actually change who we are by changing how we are," he said. "Studies are showing that we can change the architecture of our brains. That we can change the way the brain responds to its environment, and how robustly it can deal with negative emotional states." Just as our brain creates neural pathways to respond to stress, we can create neural pathways that increase our ability to focus, to be in the moment, and increase our awareness, our openness to others, and our compassion.

When our citizens develop these skills, I'm certain our country will be healthier. Too many people doing some of the toughest jobs in our country—teaching our children, taking care of the sick, responding to crises—burn out and leave their careers while they're still in the prime of life. Not only is this bad for them but it's also costly for our nation. Not only that, but high stress has made our country an angrier place, a less civil and congenial place. When we have differences, we so often seem to negotiate them not through spirited debate or competition but rather through mean-spirited rancor and threats.

We not only need to reduce our stress. We have to become kinder, for the sake of our own survival.

⌒

Even Darwin suggested that togetherness and cooperation, like the kind we saw initially on 9/11, is positively adaptive for human beings. According to the evolutionary psychologist Dacher Keltner—a professor at the University of California at Berkeley who studied under the leading researcher on human emotion in our time, Paul Ekman—in his book *Born to Be Good: The Science of a Meaningful Life*, "survival of the kindest" is as important a principle as "survival of the fittest." I visited with Keltner and his team from the Greater Good Science Center that he directs at Berkeley. With his cool and cheery demeanor, he reminded me of a surfer dude, but I soon discovered the serious scientist within. Over dinner he talked about how we have built-in mechanisms that might prioritize the gains of others over those of the self, and transform others' gains into our own. Keltner tells us in his book that this cost-benefit reversal turns our inner compass in the direction of cooperation, of *benefitting the other as well as the self.* It forgives. It's willing to cooperate at the first sign of cooperative action on the part of the other, even after long runs of mean-spiritedness.

The emotions that promote a meaningful life, according to Keltner, are organized to take an interest in the welfare of others, not merely to look for negative information. One of these is *compassion*, which makes us feel we are connected to other people. We care about what they care about. They need us and we're willing to be needed by them. Another such emotion is *awe*, which "shifts the very contents of our self-definition away from the emphasis on personal desire and preferences and toward that which connects us to others." Neurochemicals, like oxytocin, and regions of the nervous system related to these emotions promote trust and long-term devotion. "We have been designed," Keltner says, "to care about things other than the gratification of desire and the maximization of self-interest."

To make the point further, Keltner was eager to talk to me about the vagus nerve: the bundle in our chest that helps us communicate with others by controlling gaze and head movements. It also slows our heart rate and helps with digestion and immune response. According to his team's research, Dacher told me enthusiastically, "When people feel compassion and awe, this ancient mammalian bundle of nerves fires. We are wired to be kind."

At Stanford University, the Center for Compassion and Altruism Research and Education (CCARE), under the direction of the neurosurgeon Dr. James Doty, is doing studies and conducting courses that show that compassion and altruism can be cultivated through disciplines and practices that extend our mindfulness by asking us to place our increased attention on the needs of others. Paradoxically, that brings about greater contentment and well-being in ourselves. It turns out that caring for and about others makes *us* happier. How about that? Maybe that's why my grandparents were so happy.

⌒

A two-page magazine advertisement I saw promoting asset management services shows a young girl who aspires to greater and greater heights of wealth and possession—some people's version of the American Dream. The slogan is "You never stop growing." Her life is measured by her move to ever grander living spaces, ever larger carbon footprints, from crib to bunk bed to her own room, and so on, as illustrated by a growth chart written on a pillar she is leaning against. The highest point on the growth chart—the greatest aim in her pursuit of happiness in America—is a "ten-acre ranch."

We've been led to believe that getting more and greater stuff and territory will make us truly happy. What we are learning from the scientific research on mindfulness and well-being affirms the age-old wisdom that true happiness lies in the strength we have within, not what we collect and acquire. As Jesus said in the famous biblical passage, "Blessed are the meek, for they shall inherit the earth."

WHAT YOU CAN DO

- If you believe that the scientific findings I've mentioned here could help our country understand what mindfulness can do, write your congressional representative or senator. Encourage them to support funding for the National Institutes of Health, which distributes grants to researchers like the ones we just talked about.

- Ask around to find out if anyone at the medical school nearest you is doing research on mindfulness. Encourage them to give a talk at your local Y, PTA, or public library.

- Find out if your child's science teacher knows about the neuroscience of mindfulness.

- Keep a lookout for articles reporting scientific studies about mindfulness in the papers and on the internet, and share them with influence makers in your community, your children's teachers, your doctor, your spiritual adviser, and others.

CHAPTER 4

HOW MINDFULNESS CAN INCREASE OUR CHILDREN'S ATTENTION AND KINDNESS

The faculty of voluntarily bringing back a wandering attention, over and over again, is the very root of judgment, character, and will. . . . An education which should improve this faculty would be the education par excellence.

— WILLIAM JAMES

You may remember from Chapter 1 how our son, Mason, talked about how much he likes tae kwon do. One day Mason was working on his reading with his mom, who herself is a fourth-grade teacher. She takes great care with her children's education. He was practicing reading aloud, and he obviously was having a hard time. I happened to be visiting with them, so when he started crying, I decided to ask him what was wrong and he said, with tears streaming down his beet-red face, "This book is just too hard for me!"

I knew that Andrea wouldn't force him to read a book that was beyond his capability, so it seemed to me he might be getting all balled up emotionally, making it difficult for him to read something that he was actually capable of reading. It reminded me of the difficulties I had with reading as a child and how stressed out I could get about it, which just made it even harder.

Mason was tired, fussy, and upset with himself for not reading well. His pride was hurt, and he felt his inability to read meant that he wasn't smart. As his emotions got more out of control, each time he tried again to read, he quickly gave up. Andrea needed a break, so I asked if I might try to help out.

I sat down with him, not knowing what I might say but just wanting to ease his frustration. It occurred to me that some things I'd been learning about mindfulness and schoolchildren might do some good here. At least it couldn't hurt. I'd learned that children benefit from getting a handle on what's happening in their brains, as a precursor to doing short practices that can help calm their emotions and increase their attention.

So after he stopped crying, I asked him if he knew what had just happened to him.

"No," he said as he intently watched my face waiting for a possible answer.

"Well, there is this little part of your brain right here behind your forehead." I tapped the right side of his forehead with my finger like I was tapping my finger to the beat of some music.

"You feel that?" I asked.

"Yeah," he answered.

"Right behind that bone is a part of your brain that helps you read." He paid closer attention. "And farther back there is a part of your brain that helps you control your emotions." His eyes squinted as he looked at me. "I bet you started off reading a little bad, but the more you got upset, the more you couldn't read. And then you got so upset you couldn't read at all?"

He sheepishly nodded his head yes. Then I started clowning a little and using my hands to demonstrate. One hand played the role of the part of the brain that helps in reading, and the other played the role of the brain governing emotions. I explained that when he got all revved up, the emotional part of the brain interfered with the part that helps him read. I made some weird noises and had one hand take over the other hand. Again and again, I made a silly noise and let the "emotional" hand dominate the "reading" hand. He started to smile, and I smiled back.

Mason had already been following his breath for short periods, almost as a kind of a game. He even has a cushion to sit on to practice. So I reminded him that when he follows his breath he can calm his body and mind. He took a deep breath and then just sat quietly and followed his breath for a few minutes. He decided to give the reading another try. It was not perfect, but he attacked the words, broke them down, and sounded them out. After just a sentence or two he got so excited he shouted, "Mommy, Mommy, I'm reading!" He finished the story and got better and better as he read. Before I left, I again reminded him that he can calm his brain down whenever he wants.

This is not the end of the story, Andrea told me. The next evening, when the time came for him to do his day's reading assignment, he said, "Mommy, can I sit on my cushion before we read?"

"Of course," she said. She did some simple mindfulness practices together with him for about five minutes. He went on to read almost flawlessly, the best he ever had. She told me it choked her up to see her son overcoming his emotional struggle and moving swiftly through the words.

⌒

A young child who can regulate his emotions is a child who will do better in school. Why not teach all of our children this simple, tremendously powerful technique to help increase their capacity to learn and regulate their own emotions? We don't need more gadgets or fly-by-night programs in our school systems. If we teach children to follow their breath—and return to it when they get distracted—we are teaching them how to concentrate. Over time they will increase their ability to mobilize their attention. Isn't that what teachers and parents have been screaming to kids forever: "Pay attention!"? With mindfulness, we can teach them *how* to pay attention.

My brief, simplified explanation to Mason about what was happening to his brain is based on the kind of research I talked about in Chapter 3—the brain-imaging work I saw firsthand when I visited Richie Davidson's lab. As he observed, intense emotional states interfere with the area of the brain that we need for executive functions, like focusing on a task, making decisions, and solving problems. Mindfulness training helps us develop the ability to see the disturbing thought patterns and disengage from them by returning to the present moment. By training our children in methods for returning to the natural focus we find in the present, we teach them how to help their conscious mind override their unconscious mind. With a daily practice of following the breath, even for short periods, children can learn to not "take the bait" of the distracting and often negative thoughts and stories the mind creates. They can begin to develop an inner eye that sees the stories that are about to carry them away. Instead of getting hooked into them, upset, and ripped out of the present moment, they can see the story line, let it go, and return to their breath and the present moment. When the brain finds focus in the present moment, Richie told me, it is likely that the brain is releasing a chemical, a neurotransmitter called acetylcholine that produces calm and increased focus. It's that feeling when you've entered what athletes call *the zone*, and you're so in tune with what you're doing that it doesn't seem like work. You enjoy it.

When Mason had his meltdown, he had taken the bait. His unconscious mind took off and he followed it. He followed his made-up story of how he was a bad reader, how he was not smart. If he did not read well, he told himself, no one would like him and God knows what else.

What happened when he took his little mindfulness break?

His brain got off the negative narrative that made him so upset. The knowledge of how his brain actually works helped him understand what happened. He brought his attention to his breathing, followed it as it flowed in and out, and then, as his brain released acetylcholine, he was able to calmly resume reading.

~

Should every school district teach this approach to every student in the country? It seems so simple and inexpensive, and its effectiveness is backed by scientific research. What would it look like if we created a curriculum around this research? In fact, several organizations around the country have developed curricula for teaching mindfulness and what is called social and emotional learning (SEL). Social and emotional learning focuses on developing emotional resilience skills that when lacking, can cause poor education outcomes and disrupt the school environment. A student having regular tantrums, bullying, or being bullied is not going to get a good education.

The Collaborative for Academic, Social, and Emotional Learning (CASEL) out of Chicago is one of the leading organizations promoting SEL and forms of education that build resilience in children. The Hawn Foundation is another, and Cultivating Awareness and Resilience in Education (CARE) at the Garrison Institute in upstate New York is yet another. These initiatives have produced very encouraging results with teachers and students. Their programs focus on developing self-awareness, self-management, social awareness, relationship skills, and responsible decision-making.

One of the topics Jon Kabat-Zinn and I discussed in depth after the Power of Mindfulness retreat was parenting and education. Jon and his wife, Myla, wrote a book on mindful parenting called *Everyday Blessings*, because the education and upbringing of children are of significant interest to them. Jon told me that one of the leading figures in the area of mindfulness and schools is Linda Lantieri, who has been an educator in New York City for more than 40 years. She is one of the most influential people in CASEL, which I learned about for the first time that day. Jon also gave me the book Linda wrote together with Daniel Goleman: *Building Emotional Intelligence: Techniques to Cultivate Inner Strength in Children.* After reading just a few pages as a member of a House subcommittee that deals with education, I knew I had to meet Linda.

Linda was asked by the September 11th Fund to help the schools in the Ground Zero area of Manhattan recover from the trauma of the event. She decided to integrate the teaching of mindfulness practices with SEL, which was already happening in many schools, and give these skills first to the teachers and parents, and then to the students. One can only imagine the trauma a child would have experienced being close to the Twin Towers on that fateful day. Linda understands that many children experience traumas in their daily lives that are almost as intense. They grow up in low-income, high-crime areas. They often live in households that have experienced job loss or in which one or both parents are abusive. Over time these stressors have a debilitating effect. These children see so much bad that their brains are in a constant state of anxiety. They're frustrated the way Mason was when he was trying to read, but much more so. The stress for many children is constant, and it is often intensified through physical abuse. Based on her experience in the Ground Zero project, Linda decided to start the Inner Resilience Program. The program that Linda started focused on cultivating the inner lives of students, teachers, and schools by integrating social and emotional learning with mindfulness practice—not only for the disadvantaged, but for all children, since every child in America in the 21st century lives with lots of pressures. (After 15 years of operation, Linda and her team decided to wind down the Inner Resilience Program in 2017, assess what it had learned, share it with others, and allow Linda to expand her work into other areas.)

Mason has all the advantages in school and in life, yet stress can still decrease his ability to learn. I had all the advantages too, and stress made it hard for me to read. No one ever presented an alternative. Linda and her many colleagues remain committed to giving our children tools that help them find inner resilience and thrive amid these pressures.

I was so impressed with Linda Lantieri's work that I invited her to testify before our House Appropriations Subcommittee on Education. After learning more from her about what SEL combined with contemplative practice can do for children, my committee directed almost $1 million in federal money to two schools in my district to implement mindfulness and SEL and evaluate their effectiveness.

I attended the fourth day of a five-day training that Linda was giving to the teachers in our Youngstown-Warren program. I'll never forget walking into the hotel conference room that day. Linda asked me to stop by and say hello. I must admit I was a bit apprehensive. This SEL/mindfulness program for these schools had been completely my idea. I had talked the superintendents into doing it. Now I had to go see if the teachers were actually responding to it. I was concerned some of the teachers would view this as a well-meaning, do-gooder, tree-hugger approach to teaching that would never work in the heart of inner-city Youngstown. Or that the Warren teachers didn't have time for yet another program that took time away from their already overburdened lives. As I noticed these thoughts, I started to do a little walking meditation. I focused on my breath and feet as they touched the ground. I focused on not bringing my insecurities to this moment and on just dealing with the situation as it presented itself. I was glad I did, because what I saw inspired me and opened my heart.

As I entered the conference room I could feel a palpable sense of calm. The teachers were on a break and it was quiet. There was not the kind of chatter one would normally hear at a conference coffee break. No one was looking at their watch or the clock. I saw Linda in the lobby and asked her how it was going. "Amazing," she said. The training really resonated with the teachers. I asked a few of the other trainers, and they all said the same thing. Then Linda introduced me to share a few words, which I did briefly.

As I finished up, Linda asked me to stay for one of the exercises. She pulled out a large stuffed globe. Next she asked the teachers to raise their hands and share with the group of 60 teachers, and me, an awareness they had discovered during the week of training. Teacher after teacher stood up and was tossed the globe, and as they held it, poured their heart out. One said, "I've already started treating my own children differently." Another said, "I've been looking for something like this for thirty years." Yet another said she finally realized her problem was that she never took time to care for herself . . . so how could she possibly be there for her kids? She was excited to start school the next week. Another said she felt reborn as a teacher, returning to why she got into the profession in the first place. I couldn't believe what I was hearing. I had a huge lump in my throat thinking that what had just transpired in that week could transform our schools and our community. Then one of the three male teachers caught the globe. I braced for some criticism and my neck stiffened. Maybe this did not touch the men in the room the way it did the women.

I was wrong. He talked about going to his son's soccer game the night before, and he said that he was actually *at* the soccer game. His mind was not somewhere else. He was with his son. He said he looked at the beautiful blue sky and the clover grass and found a real sense of peace. It hit me how potent SEL/mindfulness is. It even resonates with ordinary American guys like me and the male teachers I met in Warren, Ohio.

We couldn't get these kinds of results without lots of local support, and when it comes to public education, union support is vital. Two of the biggest advocates for our local SEL program were the head of the teachers' union in Youngstown at the time, Will Bagnola, and his wife, Lori. Youngstown has a long history of union membership. As the industrialization of this country grew in the steel belt, unions protected and empowered workers, and made the workplace safer and more humane. The unions were made up of hard-nosed, hard-working people who were willing to fight, and even die, for social justice, fair wages, and safe working conditions. Why would a 50-year-old lifelong union man be so high on SEL/mindfulness? It's because he carries with him the heart of the industrial union movement: better lives for everyone. Will agrees with me that SEL makes the workplace a safer and more humane place. The face of the union movement is changing, and I believe Will is going to be lauded as one of the most progressive leaders because of his support and advocacy of SEL/mindfulness. And other unions will follow Youngstown's lead. Eventually, unions will be negotiating for SEL/mindfulness throughout the country.

⌒

Goldie Hawn needs no introduction. We all know her from TV and movies in the role she performs as a saucy, ditzy blonde. In person, she is an intellectual, inspirational force in the world of SEL and mindfulness in the schools. She is strategic and savvy, and has become an articulate spokesperson for the movement. I met her in my Washington office in the spring of 2009. We became fast friends and discovered a shared passion for getting mindfulness and SEL implemented in as many schools as possible, if not every school. Her Hawn Foundation developed a detailed curriculum called MindUP, which has been published by Scholastic. MindUP is now training teachers and staff in schools and youth service organizations, like the YMCA and the Boys and Girls Clubs, in 12 states. It's also operating in Canada, the United Kingdom, Serbia, Mexico, Hong Kong, Australia, and New Zealand. Goldie is now known around the world as much for her work with schoolchildren as for her acting roles. She invited me to visit one of her schools in Virginia. So I did. And I was deeply impressed.

As I pulled up to the school, Goldie was just getting out of her car. I had a moment of being starstruck. She had made me laugh a million times growing up, and her partner, Kurt Russell, delivered a powerful performance when he played Herb Brooks, the U.S. Olympic hockey coach, in one of my all-time favorite movies, *Miracle*. I later met Kurt at a MindUP event and was delighted to see how much he supported Goldie in this work. I found it inspiring that they would use their celebrity in such a positive and transformational way.

As we walked into this grade school in Northern Virginia, it seemed like any other reasonably good school in America. It was clean and relatively new. The teachers greeted us warmly, and it was clear Goldie had been hands-on with the personnel at the school. In my eight years as a congressman and two years as a state senator, I have visited many schools and seen a variety of educational innovations. I was keenly interested in what we were about to see.

As we walked down the narrow hall, we were shown the children's artwork taped to the wall. It had all the essential elements of a normal elementary school art project: construction paper, yarn, glue, and crayon. But this project was different. The construction paper was divided into two sides to show the different states of the brain's amygdala. One side was constructed to show an amygdala in its normal state as an almond-shaped set of neurons buried deep in the brain; the other side showed what the amygdala looks like when we get upset. This was blowing my mind. Except for the fact that they were created with yarn or crayons, I never would have guessed that these depictions of brain states were done by elementary school kids.

The MindUP curriculum explains how the amygdala is a filter that regulates our emotional states. And when a person, a child in this case, is in a positive emotional state, the filter is open and able to send information to the prefrontal cortex, where our higher-level thinking and reasoning take place. When the amygdala is stressed, information is not transferred. That information is processed directly by the amygdala, which orders an automatic response to protect the owner: fight, or flight, or freeze. The higher-order thinking skills of the prefrontal cortex are shut down. No reasoned judgment occurs when we're under high levels of stress. The stress Mason put on himself when he had difficulty reading—without any significant outside stimulus such as an attacking animal—shut down his prefrontal cortex. No prefrontal cortex, no reading. No prefrontal cortex, bad decision making. Goldie and I kept walking.

The first classroom we entered was the first grade. The children were extremely well behaved as they sat on the carpeted floor. The teacher was seated on a small chair in front and seemed to have complete command of the classroom. After a few brief introductions, we sat down and the teacher asked for a volunteer to show us what their amygdala does if someone pushes them on the playground. A young African American boy was called on. He stood up and started shaking and waving his arms in the air and swinging his hips as if he were playing with a hula hoop. He was going nuts, the way his amygdala would if he were in a state of fear. No information was going to the prefrontal cortex under that scenario. And probably lots of bad decisions would be made. We all laughed with the boy. He seemed to enjoy the spotlight, and a huge smile came over his face. He sat back down. The teacher picked another student to show us what the amygdala did in a positive emotional state. A beautiful, elegant girl with dreadlocks stood up. She closed her eyes, took a deep breath, and brought calm to her entire body. Her amygdala was relaxed in a positive state and could relay information to the prefrontal cortex. This meant better decision-making, better access to short-term memory, and ease of focus.

MindUP and other programs like it are based on the understanding that awareness of how your brain is working is the first step to learning how to control it, how to better regulate and guide your emotional responses. We need our emotions, of course. The goal is not to become emotionless, like Data or Spock on *Star Trek*. The point is to channel our emotions into productive use. We need to be able to lead them, not be led by them.

It's like a golfer who becomes aware of a flaw in her swing. The awareness alone opens up the possibility of regaining control of the swing. The next step is addressing the problem by learning a new technique or approach. But no adjustment of her emotional reaction or her golf swing or her negative habitual patterns can occur without an awareness of what caused her to lose focus and what kinds of effects that has. As children become more aware of how their brain actually works, it opens the door for their being able to shape their responses and regain control of their bodies and emotions. All parents want their children to act properly and to "be nice." Mindfulness is an effective way to teach kids how to first recognize, and then properly handle, their emotions. Mindfulness techniques calm the amygdala and allow information to be processed in the prefrontal cortex, from which a child can make good decisions and *respond*. From the amygdala, the child would only *react*.

Our next stop was a second-grade class. Goldie and I sat down with about 15 students and a few adults. The room was completely silent, which surprised me, given the size of the class. This is a school district that has gang and drug problems, reports of domestic abuse, and other issues associated with substandard socioeconomic conditions. Our instructions from the teacher were to sit in silence and observe our breath for a couple of minutes. She rang a chime to start us off. A few minutes later we opened our eyes, and the teacher had each of us mention to the class what was "on your mind" during the silent time. The first student said she was concerned about a test she had coming up. The next few had some pretty conventional thoughts for second-graders. One was thankful for her teacher. Another was thinking about lunch and recess. Then it was the turn of a young boy who hesitated as he put his head down. The teacher encouraged him to share. The silence in the room became palpable again, and all eyes were on this young boy. He said, and this is seared into my memory, "I'm worried that my older brother didn't come home last night." That hit me like a ton of bricks, and I tried desperately to keep my composure. No kid his age should have to worry that his brother might be killed. How on earth would this child be able to concentrate in school? What state was *his* amygdala in? How could he focus on the task at hand? How was he going to be able to draw from his working memory? What would his response be if someone pushed him on the playground? How many detentions and suspensions would this kid get? How many days of school would he miss?

The upside was that this child not only got the thought out of his mind, but he knew he was having that thought. How many of us go through life and never pause to see what is causing us so much pain? How many of us never developed that inner eye to see the thoughts in our head? I took solace in the fact that this young boy could at least identify what he was thinking, which is the first step to dealing with it courageously. His teachers and classmates now also knew what he was going through and could be sensitive to his situation. Imagine what happens to a kid who pushes that pain down inside himself day in, day out. A world of hurt is built up, and negative thoughts and experiences just keep compounding. This can often lead to negative, antisocial behavior like violence and substance abuse. Mindfulness and SEL can help to arrest that process before it takes over a child's life.

The idea that all we need as a country is a strict focus on standardized tests is folly. Social and emotional learning combined with mindfulness gets us underneath the causes of poor performance and bad behavior. It goes to the heart of the problem and transforms young minds. We need to stop pretending that emotional states like these have no effect on learning. We know better now. We have the tools to address these problems in our schools. What are we waiting for?

⌒

I met Patricia Jennings, who goes by Tish, in May 2010 at the grand opening of the Center for Healthy Minds, headed by Richie Davidson at the University of Wisconsin–Madison. Tish has a résumé as long as your arm in education research and development as well as lots of hands-on experience. She was the founding director of a Montessori school in California, where she developed and field-tested a curriculum using a variety of contemplative techniques. Tish is associate professor of education at the Curry School of Education at the University of Virginia and an important player in the Contemplative Sciences Center there. She is also the author of *Mindfulness for Teachers: Simple Skills for Peace and Productivity in the Classroom.* At the time I met Tish, she was the director of Cultivating Awareness and Resilience in Education, the initiative of the Garrison Institute that I mentioned earlier.

The thrust of the CARE program, Tish told me, is to help teachers do their job better. Without a doubt, teaching is a rewarding profession that can bring out the best in people. All of us can remember a teacher who made a big difference in our lives. Yet teaching is also one of the most stressful professions, particularly as the classroom environments teachers are put in are filled with more and more stressed-out kids. The CARE program trains teachers in disciplines of mindfulness and awareness that enable them to discover inner resources to help them do a better job for students and create a richer classroom environment, one that fosters greater participation and learning. I was not surprised to discover that the program Tish directs is based on the same understanding of neuroscience I encountered in Linda Lantieri's and Goldie Hawn's programs.

CARE for Teachers has been pilot tested in several sites across the country—in Colorado, California, Pennsylvania, and New York. It has also been adapted to support teachers and clinical staff at a school for children who have been exposed to trauma. Fortunately, the program has received a boost with funding from the Institute of Education Sciences, the research arm of the U.S. Department of Education, to complete pilot testing in urban, suburban, and rural districts in central Pennsylvania. They are collecting data on changes in teacher well-being and classroom outcomes as a result of giving teachers access to contemplative techniques like the kind I have practiced. According to Tish, early results showed reductions in teachers' time-related stress and burnout as well as improvement in their ability to regulate their emotions. Teachers also said the climate in their classrooms improved. The next stage of the research will investigate the effects that calmer teachers may have on student learning. As we saw with the teachers taking part in the program in my district, a little attention can change lives.

Tish was talking to me about how challenging it can be for teachers to face students with emotional difficulties. Sometimes they respond to the challenge by trying to overcontrol the children. She said that sometimes teachers can even begin to resent and reject the children because their own amygdalas have gone rogue. But when they can interrupt that with a moment of mindfulness and return to awareness of the present moment, they may see what's actually going on with the child as well, instead of just seeing a "problem child," a nuisance who is ruining their day. We need to support our teachers with this kind of help. As Tish says, "If teachers can notice the emotion within their body, they can stop and make choices. Instead of seeing children with challenging behavior as problems, they can experience them as suffering human beings who need compassion. Over time, that will change how they lead their classrooms." Amen.

⌒

I want to mention a few other people and groups doing good work that I haven't treated here, simply because I haven't yet had the pleasure to meet with them and have an in-depth conversation. But I look forward to the day when I can. Susan Kaiser Greenland, author of *The Mindful Child* and *Mindful Games*, began a program in Los Angeles called Inner Kids for pre-K through grade 12 children that teaches what Susan calls the new ABCs: attention, balance, and compassion. Susan has trained teachers all over the world, and in 2011 she trained teachers in eight American cities. A study of Inner Kids' work that showed increases in children's executive function was published in the *Journal of Applied School Psychology* in 2010.

Mindful Schools, founded in Oakland, California, in 2007 by Laurie Grossman, Richard Shankman, and Megan Cowan, has created a network of educators from all 50 states and more than 100 countries, impacting more than 1.5 million children and adolescents worldwide. As much as possible, the program involves students in every grade, and the training has been presented at all levels of presecondary education. In January 2009, Mindful

Schools began adult professional training for teachers and other professionals working with children. To illustrate one of the main benefits of mindfulness, Megan Cowan likes to quote Fred Rogers, the late host of *Mister Rogers' Neighborhood* on PBS. Testifying before Congress, he said, "If we can teach children that feelings are mentionable and manageable, we will have done a great service for mental health." Cowan says that's exactly what mindfulness does for children: it offers them "access to the fundamental human capacity to pay attention to oneself, to have self-awareness."

Both these programs also work with high school students, as does Peace in Schools in Portland, Oregon, and Ashanti Branch's wonderful after-school program in Oakland, California, the Ever Forward Club. It would be great to see more programs focusing specifically on high school, since so many students lose their way in adolescence. When someone picks up that torch, I will be there to help them.

A bit more is happening in higher education. That has special meaning for me because I first discovered mindfulness in college, and various forms of mindfulness helped me through law school. It's clear that young people who are trying to navigate a higher education, who are trying to discover who they are and where they want to go in life, would be well served by learning mindfulness methods. Higher education in this country began as a deeply reflective and contemplative activity, and many professors would like to make that a key part of students' modern-day experience of college. Fortunately, the Center for Contemplative Mind in Society in Northampton, Massachusetts, has a number of programs that help students. One of the leading lights in that campaign, Arthur Zajonc, emeritus professor of physics at Amherst

College, has said, "Knowledge, from the point of view of any contemplative tradition, is not primarily object-oriented. It is epiphany or insight-oriented. It's not good enough to know *about* reality; you need to change how you *see* reality. Real education is transformation."

Another program focused primarily on college students, Koru Mindfulness at Duke University, was developed by Holly Rogers and Margaret Maytan, authors of *Mindfulness for the Next Generation*. Rogers's recent book, *The Mindful Twenty-Something*, is filled with lots of great instructions and advice for people in that critical age bracket.

Because the university is a mirror of society as a whole—all the disciplines for developing and managing our society reside there—it can be a powerful place to bring mindfulness to how we run the world: how we do architecture, city planning, social work, public health administration, government, and so on. And it can start with students. Harold Roth, who runs the Contemplative Studies Initiative & Concentration at Brown University in Providence, Rhode Island, says that he brings together "traditional academic third-person inquiry and the first-person inquiry of the great contemplative traditions." His students take part in mindfulness labs where they can study the working of their own minds. I can only say how much I wish I'd had the opportunity to do the same during my own college years.

⌒

Helping to foster real improvements in our education systems nationwide is an important goal for me. But we need to be careful, even skeptical, of new initiatives. The proof of the pudding is in the eating. The *Journal of*

Research on Educational Effectiveness evaluated 20 ethnically and economically diverse public schools in Hawaii. Ten of the schools implemented daily 15- to 20-minute lessons teaching self-management, relationship skills, and self-improvement. Participants outperformed the control group by 8.8 percent in reading and 9.8 percent in math on the national TerraNova test, and 21 percent in reading and 51 percent in math in state tests. The SEL participants also had 70 percent fewer suspensions and 15 percent less absenteeism.

A CASEL meta-analysis of reports on 213 programs for children ages 5 to 18 indicates that SEL programs improve students' social-emotional skills, attitudes about self and others, connection to school, and positive social behavior; they also reduce conduct problems and emotional distress. Students' achievement-test scores increased by 11 to 17 percentile points.

These programs work. They help children like the one at Goldie's school who was worried about his brother. He could seek refuge in his school and his peers because he felt attached to them. He learned how to calm his amygdala and is therefore learning how to deal with conflict more effectively. In effect, he's been taught the very skills that might ensure that he doesn't end up in a gang. He gets support from his school, so he does not seek that support from a gang. He is learning how to handle conflict, so he does not use violence to deal with situations. And he opens his true self for the community and does not try to hide it behind a jacket of a certain color. For a very small investment, we can prevent incredible future costs and heartaches in our communities. How much more wealth will be created because we have more intellectually developed children? How many students will we keep out of the juvenile justice system? How much crime can be prevented? How much will we save in pre-venting substance abuse? How much depression will be prevented because these kids will be able to discuss their problems with each other? How many teen suicides will be prevented because fewer children will feel isolated and alone? We are a compassionate country. We are a smart country. This needs to be reflected in our curriculum.

Children in America deserve every opportunity to fully develop their talents—and I know that's what their parents want because they talk to me about it all the time. For the future of our country, it's essential that we teach the whole child, that we enable children to benefit from simple methods that improve their learning ability. If we are to compete in a fiercely competitive global economy, we have to have every child on the field playing for us. We have fewer than 400 million people in America. We are competing against China with 1.4 billion, India with 1.3 billion, and the rest of the world. We cannot afford to lose one child because we failed to educate them and prepare them with the life skills necessary to compete in a rapidly changing environment.

We have structural problems in our country in the areas of energy, health care, economics, national secu-rity, and more. We need all of our citizens to be at the top of their game to help us address these challenges. With mindfulness and SEL, we have found techniques to enhance the performance of all of our children. Rejecting or ignoring this would be like a college football program saying they were not going to implement a weight-lifting regimen to make their players stronger. These programs are being proven successful every single day. Let's invest in this simple, cost-effective strategy. Let's implement this in all of our schools. And let's give local communi-ties the resources and expertise they need to make this a part of their schools' culture. Much is at stake. That's why in 2011 I co-sponsored a bill in Congress introduced by Judy Biggert, a Republican from Illinois, that would do just that. It's called the Academic, Social, and Emotional Learning Act. I reintroduced it in 2015.

After the financial meltdown in late 2008, we experienced the worst recession since the Depression. As a result, budgets have been tight in every school district across the country and show no signs of growing anytime soon. Many states have made severe cuts to education and other needed investments. As a public official, I am deeply concerned about our long-term budget deficits and national debt. That is why I am advocating for SEL/mindfulness. It is inexpensive and easily disseminated, it will have the support of the teachers—and most important, it works. If we implement SEL/mindfulness in our schools, we will see a significant increase in our children's test scores and good behavior. We will see a decrease in teen depression and suicides.

Mindfulness can have great benefits for our children, but it can also help us be better parents. If you bring a touch of mindfulness to parenting, you may notice that you are less inclined to immediately react negatively to something your child has done. If your stress level is decreased a bit, you may be less likely to cause an emotionally charged situation to spin out of control. If you can slow down a bit, you may find yourself appreciating the free-spiritedness and curious nature of your child more often. If you're paying closer attention and listening deeply, you may notice your kids being more willing to open up to you. You may find yourself being more affectionate to them, and this may make them more affectionate toward you. Practicing mindfulness for a few weeks won't turn someone into a perfect parent. But if we slow down and reduce our own stress, it may make home life noticeably calmer and more harmonious.

Growing up, I remember two phrases being drilled into my head from my mom, the nuns, and my other teachers: Pay Attention! and Be Nice! Well, the most frustrating part of growing up and hearing that was that no one ever showed us how to pay attention! It's not something you do automatically. It needs to be taught and practiced. Telling young kids to pay attention without teaching them how reminds me of watching young children try to play baseball for the first time. Even if they can hit the ball, they immediately run for third base. They know what to do, but until someone shows them how to get to first base, they can't play the game. So it is with paying attention. We have an obligation to do all we can for our children. Let's make our kids aware of the deep inner resources and resilience they possess. Let's develop their capacity to think and to care about each other and to know themselves better. We are on the cusp of implementing revolutionary change to our educational system. We need your help in promoting such change. The future of our country depends upon it.

WHAT YOU CAN DO

- If you're interested in getting mindfulness and SEL into your child's school, get information about these programs from the resources section at the end of this book and send it to the members of the school board and the principal.

- Write your congressional representative or senator, and suggest beefing up funding for the Institute for Education Sciences, mentioned in this chapter.

- Bring information to your parent-teacher meeting and show your children's teacher what is happening in classrooms around the country.

- Write your governor, local state representative, and state senator. Ask them if your state is promoting these cutting-edge programs. Get others involved, and start a letter-writing campaign.

- If you are a teacher, start an informal mindfulness group for your fellow teachers. Get an area in the school designated for some quiet time to recharge.

- Some teachers have a "mindful eating table" where they eat quietly in the lunchroom and invite students to join them. Try that if it interests you.

CHAPTER 5

HOW MINDFULNESS CAN IMPROVE OUR HEALTH AND OUR HEALTH-CARE SYSTEM

As human beings, we are looking for happiness that won't be so vulnerable to changing conditions, that is sustainable. That's real happiness. And we find it by cultivating our inner resources and skills.

— SHARON SALZBERG

Alex Walsh was an investment adviser in New England whose life was changed by mindfulness. The finance industry rewards being tough and strong. Finance people love the thrill of the hunt, and they're used to riding big ups and downs in the market. They keep a stiff upper lip and soldier on, and they don't usually respect people who go soft. Alex himself had fought in Vietnam. So he really knew what it meant to tough it out.

In his late 50s, Alex suffered a heart attack. His heart was blocked in four places, and he had to have stents inserted in two of them. This shocking turn of events forced him to take stock of his life, to reevaluate his lifestyle. His doctor recommended he try mindfulness. Alex took mindfulness-based stress reduction at the University of Massachusetts Medical School, home to the Center for Mindfulness in Medicine, Health Care, and Society. His instructor was Melissa Blacker, a lovely combination of gentle and tough, qualities I always admire in a teacher or trainer.

Alex told reporter Barry Boyce that when he started the training, he "entered with the attitude 'I don't know whether this is going to help me, but I'd better do it.'" When the room full of 40 people started talking about what brought them there, he recoiled. "I thought, my God, this is a big group-therapy session. This isn't what I signed up for. I'm not the sort of guy who's fond of sharing intimate information with people I do not know, but when you start listening to story after story—30 or 40 of them—you realize people are in a lot of pain, tremendous pain. It was an eye-opener for me. I've been known at times to be a little less charitable in my views of others. I realize now that a lot of them, a lot of us, are probably hurting in ways you can only begin to imagine."

As part of the course, they asked Alex if within the last week he had felt aggressive or hostile at any time. He had to reflect on what was actually happening in his body and mind when he got wound up and his stress expressed itself as inner turmoil, mentally and emotionally. In theory, his aggressive thoughts were directed outward. But in fact, he discovered that his own body and mind were taking the toll.

"Gradually, though, my stress level began to dissipate," Alex said. "I didn't exactly know why it was dissipating. It seemed to be happening as I was doing the mindfulness course. I felt much calmer and far more relaxed than I have been in a long, long time. I learned to stop and take a breath. I wouldn't have imagined my saying something like this before, but I believe in the impact of mindfulness. It's a powerful force that can make a huge difference in people's lives if they let it. Now I look at the ups and downs in the market—and in life altogether—in a way that is far healthier and more balanced."

～

Like Alex, many of us wait for a traumatic event before we look closely at our overall health. This ongoing lapse in attention is costly for us, and for our loved ones—and it's costly for the nation. Sometimes worn-out old sayings contain hard truths: an ounce of prevention *is* worth a pound of cure. And with health-care costs hitting our own pocketbooks hard and threatening to pass on crippling debt to future generations, we need to look at every way we can make ourselves healthier at low cost—and the simpler, the better.

We all realize that we have some level of control over our own health. We know smoking is bad for us. We know too much sugar or salt can have a negative effect on our health. We feel guilty about that bowl of ice cream at the end of the night. I know I do. But one of the things we sometimes fail to see is the direct effect that stress, especially chronic stress, has on our health and well-being. If we truly want to prevent unnecessary illness, we need to recognize stress as a major contributor to poor health and well-being—and ultimately to catastrophic illness.

The health-care reform we enacted in 2008, imperfect though it may have been, helped us make some important strides in the direction of prevention. The Affordable Care Act eliminated copayments for preventive disease screening for Medicare recipients and prevented insurers from charging copayments for any customer getting preventive screening. It's good we could make a step forward in encouraging people to do something to help catch diseases at their early stages.

But a growing number of distinguished health-care practitioners, like Dr. Christiane Northrup—winner of the 2010 Integrative Healthcare Visionary Award—think the current health-care system is far too focused on disease care, to the exclusion of *preventive* medicine. Even screening for diseases, while good, falls far short of promoting health in her view. The screening, as important as it is, still may be a step too late.

Finding out that your cholesterol and blood pressure are off the charts when you're 55 is better than never finding out. Medication may help you at that point. That's treating a *downstream* condition, however; it's not really creating health for ourselves. We need to start *upstream*, earlier in the process.

Northrup and others say that teaching ourselves how to handle stress more effectively is as important as screening for disease conditions. Reducing the negative impact of stress can prevent some of the diseases that would be caught at a screening. We can't have full control over all of the stress in our lives, of course, but we can reduce our conditioned, largely reactive habits and the patterns we revert to when we're confronted by perceived and real threats and challenges. We can reduce our reactivity and thereby limit the effect that stress has on our overall health.

So how *do* we foster real health for ourselves by limiting our stress reactions? How do we make ourselves more resilient and hardy in the face of so much busyness and pressure? How many times have we heard someone say, "I'm worried sick"? Now, dozens of studies are reinforcing what many of us believe intuitively: psychological and emotional stress can make us very sick. Learning to respond—rather than react—to life's challenges can help us become healthier.

⌒

One of the health-care practitioners and leaders I've had the pleasure to meet is Dr. Susan Bauer-Wu. Appointed president of the Mind & Life Institute in 2015, she was formerly director of the Compassionate Care Initiative and the Tussi and John Kluge Professor in Contemplative End of Life Care at the University of Virginia School of Nursing in Charlottesville. Susan has devoted her career to studying the effects of mindfulness practice on the health and quality of life for people living with serious illness, especially cancer, and she's written the book *Leaves Falling Gently: Living Fully with Serious and Life-Limiting Illness through Mindfulness, Compassion, and Connectedness.* She's also interested in how contemplative practices can foster resiliency in caregivers—both medical professionals and family members—and college students. Susan is a bundle of energy and enthusiasm, and healing is a family tradition. She grew up outside New York City, on Long Island, where her mother was a nurse at the huge state hospital in Central Islip. I wanted to get to know her because she has insight into how stress relates to poor health.

Susan spoke of stress as being like a drug—one we can become addicted to. We keep relying on it to get us through, instead of getting enough rest and cultivating the resiliency we need to deal with constantly shifting circumstances. I know that I—like Alex, the hard-driving Vietnam vet and financial adviser—operated like that for much of my life, until it became clear to me that I needed to pay more attention, or I would pay a big price. When I heard Susan talking about this, it occurred to me that so many of us can become like engines that run too hot. In short, our bodies get inflamed.

She says, however, that "some studies seem to be telling us that mindfulness practices can have a 'cooling' impact on the inflammatory processes in the body. Conceivably, if you begin these practices earlier, you may be able to prevent some serious chronic illnesses associated with inflammation."

Dr. Bauer-Wu also mentioned that it seems likely that mindfulness may help us by increasing our body armor. Our body is naturally resilient and will fight off invasions and infections to the best of its ability through the immune system. The psoriasis study by Kabat-Zinn and colleagues, which I mentioned in Chapter 3, also showed an increase in antibody levels after eight weeks of mindfulness training. If, in fact, mindfulness can boost our immune system to fight off disease and infection, that's real prevention at the low cost of paying more attention to what's happening in our own body. That's what you call starting *upstream*.

Developing an awareness of what is happening in our bodies in the present moment also yields obvious benefits in the form of helping us become part of the early-detection system, Susan says. We become more aware of what condition our body is in from moment to moment. We become more in tune with feelings and sensations happening in our body. Our body is always talking to us, but we don't always listen. It's like we're a child who tunes out any negative messages. "Everything's okay, Mom. Don't worry about it. I'll be fine."

So often, we tough it out like athletes. We suck it up. We play hurt. We go to work when we ought to stay home. We add another thing to a schedule that is bulging like ten pounds of potatoes in a five-pound bag. We're not really paying close attention to what's going on in the body and the damage that's taking place. Dr. Bauer-Wu says that an increased awareness of our body can help us detect problems much earlier. We can be our own best diagnostician. We may not know precisely what's wrong, but we can tell when something's up. For those of us with back problems, we know exactly when we throw our back out. We may not be hunched over right away, but we know that the stiffness and distortion are on their way— along with days or weeks of recovery.

We notice when sickness arrives because it enters our awareness. What Dr. Bauer-Wu and other health-care practitioners are telling us is that some form of cultivating our mindfulness can help sharpen our body awareness. This higher degree of awareness can help us participate in our own health care in a couple of ways. First, she told me, we may detect a possible problem before it manifests into a larger, more complex problem. All doctors tell us that it's much easier to treat something early, before it becomes full-blown and even does secondary damage. A professional singer who started practicing mindfulness as part of doing yoga noticed one night when she was having dinner in a fancy restaurant that she had a catch in her throat that seemed to extend down to her chest. Before practicing mindfulness, she would have dismissed it as heartburn, she said, but her increased awareness of her internal body function let her know it was something more serious, and that she had to give up the fancy meal and get to the hospital. Her aorta had split, and her quick attention saved her life.

Dr. Bauer-Wu also told me that increased awareness can give us insights that help us make better lifestyle decisions—both in the short term and the long term. For example, if we pay closer attention, we may notice before a cold, that we are getting run down and need a good night's sleep. So we possibly cancel an evening event, if we can, in order to get to bed early and rest. We cancel one meeting to possibly prevent ourselves from getting sick and canceling a couple of days' worth of meetings. Perhaps we haven't been eating well and we need a good meal, so we take the time to eat healthy food. And maybe that also causes us to take more time to have a leisurely paced meal with our loved ones, which can relax us (at least some of the time!). If we're more aware, we may be a bit more careful with our backs when we pick up heavy things. We may even prevent an accident at home or work, something that can debilitate us for life. Or we might begin to notice a weakness in the core muscles that support our back. So we take some time to work out and strengthen those muscles *before* we throw our back out. We also may notice other feelings in our body that should be checked out. Or we may simply feel that our stress level has been amped up because of deadlines and commitments. If we begin to notice, we can take a few minutes to cool our jets before we get too hot and inflamed. This level of awareness can benefit us, our families, and our co-workers, as well as the entire health-care system. We can make such simple, short-term lifestyle decisions if we are alert in the present moment. And this kind of early intervention can head off pain, costly doctor bills, and loss of productivity at work.

Being more aware of what's going on in our body and our mind and how the two are communicating with each other can help us make healthier *long-term* lifestyle decisions too, Dr. Bauer-Wu says. It brings some wisdom to our decision making. We get a deeper look into how our day-to-day decisions, however small they may be, connect to form patterns that create a lifestyle. At what point did we go from being active to sedentary, a condition that's the source of so many problems? When did we start looking for the closest parking space or taking the elevator up one flight? With a touch of mindfulness, we start to see how our habits, whether behavioral or mental, affect our long-term health. At the center of many eating problems, for example, Dr. Bauer-Wu told me, is a lack of noticing what you're doing in the moment. At Dr. David Ludwig's obesity clinic at Boston's Children's Hospital—called Optimal Weight for Life (OWL)—he coaxes children to mindfully taste a variety of foods to counteract unconscious gobbling. Indiana State and Duke universities conducted a joint study on binge eating, and the binge eaters who participated in a mindful eating program reduced their binging frequency by 75 percent.

⌒

Cultivating our innate mindfulness can help us get a little ahead of the game. We sharpen our inner eye and our inborn curiosity. Like a great athlete, surgeon, or teacher, we can begin to see things before they develop. This can help us to "create health for ourselves," in Dr. Bauer-Wu's words. We can free ourselves from the stuckness of constantly seeing things when it is too late. These are skills that can be learned so that we become participants in our own health care—what Jon Kabat-Zinn calls *participatory medicine.*

Participatory medicine is the guiding principle behind the Duke Integrative Medicine program, where they see over 5,000 patients a year. "We treat the whole person and have a very broad view of health and healing," says Dr. Jeff Brantley, a longtime member of the senior staff at the Duke University program. It's been my pleasure to get to know Dr. Brantley, a big teddy bear of a guy whose charm and manners would put anyone at ease—a great quality in a doctor.

"It's not only about the mind/body of a person," he told me, "but also their relationships." At Duke, they want to understand the patients' relationships to people in their community, their family, their co-workers, the food they eat, their understanding and relationship to a Higher Power—whatever that may mean to them. The caregivers in the Integrative Medicine program take stock of everything going on in the patient's life, because they know that the quality of those relationships will help determine their level of well-being. Fully engaging the patient, in addition to doing diagnostic testing, is essential to making a patient-centered approach work, Jeff told me. We're not cars that can just be taken to a quick-lube garage and have a few parts replaced, the oil changed, and then be good to go for another 5,000 miles. Nor are medical doctors and health-care practitioners like auto mechanics who can deal purely on the physical level: an outdated health-care model that is insufficient today.

We are a complicated species with perceptions, opinions, memories, inclinations, emotions, and constantly changing mental states. In a mindful nation, our citizens need an innovative health-care system that asks each person to actively *participate* in his or her own health care. This will take great courage on behalf of all of our citizens. It is difficult to look closely at what we are thinking and feeling and how those thoughts and feelings are affecting our health. Studies of mindfulness and other approaches that appreciate the close link between body and mind suggest an opportunity for each of us to play a huge role in our own health. Just as paying attention when we are driving or riding a bike can prevent accidents, increased awareness of our bodies and minds during the daily grind can help us improve our personal health and well-being. As my mom told my brother and me every single day before school, "God helps those who help themselves."

A 2003 study, and others since then, have shown that people who help themselves by practicing mindfulness seem to demonstrate positive changes in their brain function. People who work with mindfulness tend to report higher states of well-being, peacefulness, and resiliency as they cultivate certain qualities of mind like kindness, compassion, strength, equanimity, and joy. As people practice mindfulness, they are literally creating patterns within the brain and mind that can lead toward a happier, healthier life. Dr. Brantley says this shift is actually a rewiring of the brain toward "heartful qualities," and that shift leads to an improvement in people's health. And naturally the health of the community increases as individuals and their families become healthier.

The opposite is also true, Jeff says: mindlessness and negative thinking can shift our brain into fear, self-hatred, and greediness. And then these become community habits—and even underlying values. And more and more health practitioners are telling us that these closed states of mind are not simply a psychological issue alone; they have a negative effect on our health and the health of those around us.

America is a nation built on individual responsibility and self-reliance. Because of these founding principles, it makes complete sense for each of us to participate in our own health care in a meaningful way. These principles served our country so well for generations because the more responsibility a person takes for his or her own life, the less society has to bear the burden collectively. Each American relying more on his or her own capacity to prevent sickness, one citizen at a time, can be a powerful element of our campaign to reduce the heavy burden of health-care cost on our economy. Choosing health individually will create health—and wealth too—collectively.

In a recent survey of its members, the National Federation of Independent Business—the leading group representing small business—reported that out of a list of 75 challenges, the rising cost of health insurance ranked as the top problem by a considerable margin. The proportion of our economic output devoted to health costs is growing like an invasive species.

This burden takes money out of the hands of our businesspeople who would otherwise use it to reinvest in their businesses and hire our fellow citizens. If we create health for ourselves, we create wealth for ourselves and our country. What motivates a mindful approach to health is the confidence that we have the ability to care for ourselves—and that when we do fall ill, we can participate in our own healing. Our leaders need to reward such self-reliance and initiative. We need to find methods for our health-care system to reward people who actively participate in improving their own well-being. Such a tilt toward highly effective preventive approaches could be a key element in saving billons of health-care dollars.

The Preventive Medicine Research Institute in Sausalito, California, worked with eight hospitals to see whether comprehensive lifestyle changes could provide a safe, effective alternative to cardiac bypass surgery or an angioplasty. After one year, almost 80 percent of participants avoided these interventions, at a savings of almost $30,000 per patient. The direct health-care costs of conventional treatment of someone with angina are estimated to be $1 million over their lifetime. Imagine how much could be saved if mindfulness-based health interventions reduced these kinds of costs. A study of type 2 diabetes (a lifestyle-related epidemic in our nation) published in the *Journal of Internal Medicine* showed that lifestyle-change programs achieved the same beneficial result as drug treatment at a cost of $8,800 versus $29,900—a 70 percent reduction. How often do you get something for 70 percent off?

I'm delighted to say that I've made a friend in Dr. Saki Santorelli, who recently retired after serving for decades as executive director of the Center for Mindfulness in Medicine, Health Care, and Society at the University of Massachusetts Medical School, home to the MBSR program that helped Alex Walsh. Saki is a highly energetic guy who exudes a lot of warmth. He's as wiry as Jeff Brantley is bearlike. Apparently, mindfulness guys come in all shapes and sizes. I visited him at the center and was impressed with what I learned there. For nearly 40 years, the center has taken a leading role in pioneering the integration of mindfulness meditation and other mindfulness practices into mainstream medicine through clinical care; rigorous research; academic, medical, and professional education; and a wide range of programs and initiatives addressing the needs of the larger society. Eleven thousand health-care professionals and educators across five continents have participated in training programs through the center's Oasis Institute for Mindfulness-Based Professional Education. Faculty and staff there have produced more than 100 scientific papers, books, book chapters, monographs, training manuals, and abstracts about mindfulness and MBSR. From 2003 to 2013, the center hosted an international conference, "Investigating and Integrating Mindfulness in Medicine, Health Care, and Society," which I had the pleasure of attending several times along with hundreds of researchers, clinicians, and educators from around the world.

The Mindfulness-Based Stress Reduction Clinic at UMass Medical School is where mindfulness-based stress reduction began. MBSR is the most widely researched mind/body program of its type. Its approach is highly experiential, requiring ongoing, active patient participation. More than 20,000 patients completed the MBSR program at UMass, referred by more than 5,000 physicians. In 2018, UMass affirmed its commitment to researching and disseminating the potential health benefits of mindfulness by inaugurating the first Center of Mindfulness within a medical school, putting the study of mindfulness on par with the investigation of other major treatment approaches.

In the winter of 2011, Saki came to the Northeast Ohio Medical University in my district. On a snowy Monday in January, we had close to 200 doctors, psychologists, psychiatrists, professors, nurses, and hospital administrators attend our first annual mindfulness conference. It was here that I really felt the power of the latent, yet growing, mindfulness community in our nation.

One of the things I appreciate about Saki is what he has absorbed from his many years of working in a major hospital and academic health sciences center by using an approach that takes into account *both* the body and the mind. It hasn't always been easy running a clinic that teaches mindfulness practice that is, as he says, "embedded in a mainstream medical center that is nested within a larger university system that is itself nested within the State of Massachusetts." After serving tens of thousands of patients and becoming a model for medical centers all over the world, the clinic and the center provide daily evidence that cultivating mindfulness diminishes stress, increases well-being and resiliency, and reduces illness.

Mindfulness, Saki says, is not isolated to what happens inside of us. "It has real-world implications in our everyday lives," he says, "because it helps us work from *the inside out*, to use our awareness to take effective ethical action in the world. It does that by teaching us to stop, see more clearly, and *turn toward* those difficult places we find within and around us, and to stay put and allow solutions to emerge for us. By learning to pay attention, we enhance our ability to stay put rather than escape and act blindly. We understand situations more clearly, become increasingly attentive to the emergence of solutions, and act with awareness. In this way, we express our human capacity for mastery, for placing our hand on the rudder of our lives.

"It is so easy to turn away from ourselves, losing all sense of direction, no longer trusting our innate wisdom and navigational sensibilities. But if, in difficult moments, we learn to *stop* and be present, we have a chance to learn a lot."

What does the ability to stop and be present with ourselves and others have to do with health care?

Everything.

Paying attention is the source of what makes human beings effective. It's what makes a good caregiver care. It's what makes a person see how he needs to care for himself. It's what makes someone a good patient—a person who can participate fully in her own treatment. It can be the cornerstone of a health-care system that works.[3]

~

We need a system that provides incentives for health-care professionals to teach us these skills and monitor our progress. We also need to support training that promotes and increases the innate mindfulness of our health-care professionals. A study by Michael Krasner and Ronald Epstein at the University of Rochester School of Medicine, published in the prestigious *American Journal of Medicine*, showed that training primary care physicians in mindfulness reduced burnout and increased empathy. In his recent book, *Attending: Medicine, Mindfulness, and Humanity*, Dr. Epstein further documents how mindfulness can improve doctor performance. Dr. Bauer-Wu says that mindfulness and related practices can directly increase caregivers' ability to listen, to leave space to really hear what's going on with the patient in front of them, rather than letting their mind race on to the next appointment. Have you ever felt that your doctor was under such pressure that he or she was not really listening or didn't have the time to adequately pay attention to who you are and how you are? That's not good bedside manner, and it's far from what we could call empathy, which ought to be central to *giving care*.

Dr. Bauer-Wu told me that some of the same areas in our brain that are responsible for awareness of internal experience are also areas that help us empathize. When we're mindful, we are in tune with what's going on within ourselves, and we learn to empathize as well. A study published in *Family Medicine*, led by Richie Davidson's colleague David Rakel, Chair of the Department of Family & Community Medicine at the University of New Mexico, showed that when health-care practitioners are empathetic, patients get over the common cold quicker and have increased immune system function. We intuitively know the power of a compassionate caregiver—like our mother or father giving us lots of love and attention when we were sick as children—and we experience that power just beneath the surface of our conscious awareness. Now science may just be confirming our instincts.

We also need to care for our professional caregivers— our precious health-care workforce. We have a shortage of nurses in America because they are burning out. The ones who have stuck it out are constantly overworked and under strain and pressure. It's hard enough to take care of patients when you yourself are healthy; it's nearly impossible when you're completely depleted. Mindfulness training can help caregivers recharge and better deal with the pressure and strain. We want our doctors and nurses to be fully present and aware when they are trying to diagnose and treat us. We don't want them running on empty.

Make no mistake about it: medicine is a high-pressure, high-performance job. It always will be; life and death are involved. There's no way for us to turn it into a walk in the park. Professional caregivers have to deliver tough messages and consistently coax and coach us to improve our life-styles—especially if they are taking a preventive approach. On top of that, we have millions of people in this country who are under the stress of having to be caregivers for their own family members, usually elderly parents, because they can't afford professional help. They too are stressing out to the breaking point, and need our help. They're getting sick from the stress, and that's going to ultimately be another significant cost to our health-care system.

I think we need to consider innovative programs to provide assistance and stress reduction for these family caregivers. For professional caregivers, we ought to train them in a way that develops some of the inner skills attained by high-performance athletes. When I was growing up, the San Francisco 49ers—owned by the DeBartolo/York family from Youngstown—were winning Super Bowls right and left. The DeBartolos would bring their stars—Joe Montana, Jerry Rice, the coach Bill Walsh—back to Youngstown for banquets in the off-season. Once, Joe Montana was asked how he pulled off his famous game-winning performances in the last two minutes. I'm told he said that when it got tight at the end, in those clutch situations, the game actually *slowed down*. When the pressure was on, rather than amping up the stress, he would let his mind calm itself, and the world around him slowed.

Neuroscientists are telling us that if we work well with our stress, we too can employ this capability in even the most challenging situations. The trauma surgeon can have complete present-moment awareness when the heat is on in the emergency room. A nurse can be 100 percent there with us when our negative emotions about being sick come to the surface. We ourselves can learn to slow down in the middle of it all—for the good of our own health and performance. We can build up a resiliency for stress just like Joe Montana did.

My high school government teacher and coach at John F. Kennedy High School, John Gillen, is a devout Catholic who could often be seen coming in and out of the chapel in the school. He's a military veteran who sports a crew cut. He wakes up every day at 5 A.M. to do push-ups, sit-ups, and stretching. He is in touch with his inner world and has studied the work of high-performing individuals. In our first day of class he told us that average people used only 3 to 4 percent of their human potential. Who knows where these figures came from? They certainly were not precise, but the basic point rang true. I knew I wasn't bringing all my energy and capacity to the challenges I faced. His point was that with discipline and hard work we could all become peak performers and that our body and mind have so much potential and energy that go undeveloped.

More than 20 years later, that class has stayed with me. In many ways that inspiration sent me on the journey that led to mindfulness. The practice of mindfulness helped me see, though, that realizing our great potential doesn't come about by pushing ourselves to the brink of exhaustion, as I had tried to do so many times. I take the example of marathon runners or long-distance cyclists who take a day off to replenish their energy, or professional singers who rest their voice in order to tune the instrument. Mindfulness practice is a pause that refreshes.

By taking moments to pause and refresh ourselves, the mindful health-care leaders have told me, we discover deep inner reserves. When we get in touch with what's happening in our mind and body, and in our relationships, intuitively we feel healthy. As I've said, with the increasing scientific evidence that cultivating mindfulness increases our health and well-being—and can potentially reduce medical costs—it would be irresponsible of me as a congressman serving the people of Ohio and the United States not to find a way to study its effectiveness and increase its presence in our healthcare system.

As Coach Gillen taught, we Americans have to each take part in this development. We have to love and care for ourselves enough to recognize that the easy answer usually does not work. Cultivating our mindfulness is simple, but it is not easy. It takes time and work. But the results are worth it. Mindful, preventive medicine is about taking charge of our own health, about improving the health of the country by improving our own health—and about saving potentially billions of dollars from our health expenditures. Studies have shown for years that with a minor commitment we can affect our health and well-being in a positive way.

Of course, hurt, pain, and suffering will not disappear. Mindful approaches are not quick fixes or magic formulas. We can't buy our solutions off a late-night infomercial. Being mindful takes discipline and resolve. It takes great courage to turn toward difficulty, to be curious about it instead of resisting it, to peel one layer of the onion and look a bit deeper, including at the destructive or negative emotions that may be the source of ill health. But if we face them with dignity and awareness and simple inquisitiveness, we can shift our state of mind. Caregivers like Christiane Northrup, Susan Bauer-Wu, Jeff Brantley, Saki Santorelli, and many others too numerous to mention see patients day after day who prove to them how much capacity we have to take charge of our own health. And when we show some good old-fashioned American self-reliance, we lower the burden on the health-care system while becoming healthier ourselves.

Our health has its ups and downs, to be sure, but more than one person I've talked to who practices mindfulness has compared it to The Beach Boys favorite watersport: When you're on the ocean, they say, you can't stop the waves, but you can learn how to surf.

What You Can Do

- Let your doctor know about some of the health benefits of mindfulness.

- Write your representatives in state government and encourage them to include mindfulness training at your state-funded medical and nursing schools.

- Bring information to a nursing home or hospital where a family member is being cared for, and encourage the staff to give mindfulness a try to guard against burnout.

- Help start a mindfulness group for stressed-out family caregivers at a nursing home or hospital.

- Encourage your employer—or employers you work with—to have mindfulness included in the company's wellness program.

- See if your Y or health club would be interested in sponsoring a mindfulness class or local library.

CHAPTER 6

HOW MINDFULNESS CAN IMPROVE PERFORMANCE AND BUILD RESILIENCY FOR OUR MILITARY AND FIRST RESPONDERS

Mind fitness training is applicable to everything you do, whether at home with family or at work in the Marine Corps. It can be used for elite athletes, military, IBM executives—anyone who has any type of stress.

— MARINE CORPS MAJOR JIM TOTH

Often, when I'm working in Washington, citizens from Ohio will come to Capitol Hill to advocate for reforms, better regulation, funding, or legislation. A few years ago I shared a nice Italian dinner with a group of union leaders who work at hospitals in my district. We were telling stories, laughing, and having a good time.

Toward the end of the evening, one of the nurses came from the other end of the table and sat next to me. She began to tell me about her son who had done several tours of duty in Iraq. She was worried about him now that he was stateside. He was acting strangely, and his relationship with the rest of his family was getting strained. He was out of work but afraid to seek veterans' benefits because he didn't want to be diagnosed with post-traumatic stress disorder (PTSD, or PTS, as many military caregivers have started to call it, dropping the word *disorder*). He felt that label would hurt his chances of getting a job. I had been an outspoken critic of the war in Iraq from the very beginning, but that was of little relevance now. She wanted me to know just how much of a toll the war was taking on our warriors and their families.

What really struck me, though, is what she said after her general comments. Her son did not simply do an important job for his country and return to normal life; instead, he seemed changed in some fundamental way. He was seething with suppressed anger, and was violent toward himself and possibly toward others. This nurse and mother looked me in the eyes, put her hand on my arm, and as her eyes welled with tears she said, "I didn't raise a killer." Her words left me speechless. I felt the same kind of deep pain as when I stood with the father whose son had committed suicide in the backyard after returning from the war. Words don't help much at times like these. All I could do was hug her.

The breadth and depth of the pain caused by our wars in Iraq and Afghanistan hit me hard that night. This woman obviously had a sense of the complex, stressful, and life-threatening situations at the root of her son's problems. Those highly charged emotional events tend to stay vivid in our memories for a lifetime. And the body doesn't easily forget trauma either. It retains it just beneath the surface.

Unfortunately, this scenario is too common in America: a returning soldier struggles to bounce back from the mental and physical stress endured during multiple deployments to a war zone. As I indicated in Chapter 1, our military's own statistics show that we are losing this struggle. The suicide rate for veterans is estimated at 20 per day—one every 70 minutes. On average, every third day in 2016, an Army service member took his or her own life. In 2008, during the height of the wars in Iraq and Afghanistan, the Marine Corps lost more of its members to suicide than they had lost in total since the wars began. Around the same time, the Pentagon released a report showing that half of returning National Guard and reservists, 38 percent of soldiers, and 31 percent of Marines reported mental health problems. The statistics can be compiled, but the deep grief these situations have caused in our communities cannot be quantified. Our nation has a broken heart, and most of us do not realize it, while the families of the fallen are left to pick up the pieces.

Most Americans share the idea that war is to be avoided whenever possible. It is a last resort, a final action that—if it must be taken—prevents even greater harm. We must make every conceivable effort to avoid war and to work for the prevention of future war. Nevertheless, given the fact that we still have thousands of troops involved in conflicts around the globe and the chance that war may happen again, what do we do to try to decrease the level of pain war causes? What tools can we give our troops to help them overcome the stressors and challenges of war? What do we do to help protect our troops' physical and psychological well-being so that they not only can bounce back but can continue to lead rewarding lives and contribute their considerable abilities to our society once they come home? What techniques can we teach our troops that will reduce costly and tragic battlefield errors like friendly fire, collateral damage, and noncombatant deaths?

～～

Elizabeth Stanley represents the ninth generation of her family to serve in the U.S. Army. In 1996 she left the service with the rank of captain, following postings in Korea and Germany and two deployments as a peacekeeper in the Balkans. After her military service, she earned an M.B.A. from the MIT Sloan School of Management and a Ph.D. in government from Harvard; she is now associate professor of security studies at Georgetown University's Walsh School of Foreign Service.

Since I've served on both the Defense Appropriations Subcommittee and the House Armed Services Committee, I made it my business to get to know Liz, whom I now count as a friend and colleague. She has the indomitable spirit of a warrior combined with a very warm heart. She understands military service as making selfless sacrifice on behalf of one's nation, being willing to do what is asked because of one's oath to serve. In turn, she believes we owe it to our troops to prepare them both physically and mentally for the enormous challenge that we citizens ask them to face on our behalf.

Stanley knew that a warrior's mind fitness is an ancient ideal that is now being supported by science; it is measurable and can be cultivated through training. She argues that millennia of warrior traditions have all focused on training two qualities: wisdom and bravery. *Wisdom* is defined as the ability to see clearly how things are, not how we want them to be, and then to use that information to make the most effective decision in the moment. *Bravery*, according to Stanley, is the ability to stay present with any experience, even an extremely difficult one, without needing it to be different. Historically, she told me, warrior traditions used a variety of practices to cultivate these two qualities and the use of mindfulness to train soldiers follows in the lineage of these traditions.

For Liz, mindfulness has been central to her approach to dealing with the effects of the stress from her military service, and it is an important element of her research into alternatives to current approaches to national security. "My research," she writes, "has focused on the United States' overreliance on technology in national security, a cultural tendency born from the desire to feel certain, in control, and safe. This tendency has led to a devaluation of human-centric approaches to security, especially in terms of providing troops with skills to remain balanced, nonreactive, and clear-seeing, despite the extreme stress, uncertainty, and confusion of the counterinsurgency environment."

As we know from our discussion in the previous chapter, stress has a damaging effect on our physical and psychological well-being. For a war fighter placed in life-and-death situations, stress levels are amplified to the extreme. Add several tours to the war zone without sufficient intervals of downtime, witnessing loss of life and chaos, living with long-term sleep deprivation, and being away from family, and you have a prescription for chronic stress that degrades cognitive abilities and operational effectiveness. Our body responds to high levels of stress by releasing heavy doses of the hormone cortisol. Cortisol helps us deal with the stress, but over time it has a deleterious effect on the body and mind. A U.S. Army study of troops who served in Iraq showed that overall they were "highly likely to show subtle lapses in memory and an inability to focus." Liz Stanley adds that "other studies of military environments have found substantial degradation in cognitive performance when subjects experience sleep deprivation and other environmental stressors." When troops must make instantaneous life-and-death decisions, any depletion of their ability to focus or to remember who is who, can be disastrous.

These are not our grandparents' wars, as horrible as those were. These wars are being fought much differently. They usually take place in urban areas, and the enemy is dressed in civilian clothes and looks very similar to our allies.

In modern warfare, where technology dominates, many of the shots are fired from a faraway place. But the people making these decisions have another kind of stress more common to civilians—stress via information overload. A January 2011 *New York Times* article highlights how everyday problems familiar to office workers—being too busy or overloaded with information—can turn tragic in the military context:

> When military investigators looked into an attack by American helicopters last February that left 23 Afghan civilians dead, they found that the operator of a Predator drone had failed to pass along crucial information about the makeup of a gathering crowd of villagers.
>
> But Air Force and Army officials now say there was also an underlying cause for that mistake: information overload.

At an Air Force base in Nevada, the drone operator and his team struggled to work out what was happening in the village, where a convoy was forming. They had to monitor the drone's video feeds while participating in dozens of instant-message and radio exchanges with intelligence analysts and troops on the ground.

There are serious consequences for our troops' health and well-being—and for our country's goal of wanting to win hearts and minds—if they are not properly trained to handle the intense volume of rapidly transmitted information they are subject to. One soldier commented in the article that he uses a classified instant-messaging system showing as many as 30 different chats with commanders at the front, troops in combat, and headquarters at the rear. And he is hearing the voice of a pilot at the controls of a U-2 spy plane high in the stratosphere: "I'll have a phone in one ear," he told the reporter, "talking to a pilot on the headset in the other ear, typing in chat at the same time and watching screens. . . . It's intense." These soldiers report that their brain hurts when they leave work at night. Whether it's on the actual field of battle or thousands of miles away, the stress and information overload render our warriors less able to make sound decisions. In the short term, this leads to the shock and trauma of battlefield errors. In the long term, a deadly mistake on the battlefield can weigh on a soldier for life and lead to severe PTS, alcohol and drug abuse, domestic violence, divorce, and, all too often, suicide. Conflict situations have always and everywhere required taking a lot of information into account and making instantaneous decisions. Therefore, we must give our troops the most practical and effective training, training that enhances their ability to respond to and recover from the complex demands of 21st-century battles.

"The military," Stanley says, "needs to be able to mix offensive, defensive, and stability operations conducted along multiple lines of operation, without the benefit of a clearly demarcated 'frontline.' . . . Service members must navigate morally ambiguous situations with balance and nonreactivity, while drawing on stores of cultural awareness to 'win hearts and minds.'"

Her personal experiences combined with her professional research have led her to conclude that a blending of mindfulness and other related mind/body training could help soldiers and Marines develop a kind of mental fitness to "cope with the physiological and psychological effects of extreme or prolonged stress." She defines *mind fitness* as "having a mind with highly efficient capacities for mental agility, emotional regulation, attention, and situational awareness (of self, others, and the wider environment). Just as physical fitness corresponds to specific enhancements in the body, mind fitness may correspond to enhancements in specific brain structures and functions that support these capacities." One of the key aspects of mental fitness, as we discussed in Chapter 3, is "working memory" capacity, the ability to keep relevant information in the forefront of your mind while letting go of immaterial and distracting information. Having a stronger working memory capacity would obviously benefit someone operating in the midst of chaos. It would help them keep themselves and others safe. It would allow them to respond, not necessarily simply react—or overreact. Our working memory can degrade if we are overloaded. We call it a meltdown, such as the one Mason was going through when he found it tough to read. Our working memory capacity can also be increased through training, which is why mind fitness training is potentially so important for people in the military, police, firefighters, first responders to natural disasters, and others who work in high-stress environments that require taking in and managing a great deal of information in short time frames.

When people have higher working memory capacity, they can pay better attention, solve problems more readily, and have more fluid intelligence—they *use* facts rather than just *know* them. Those with strengthened working memory capacity also suffer less from emotionally charged thoughts and are more capable of letting those thoughts go and of reappraising emotions when needed.

When people have low working memory capacity, they have poorer academic achievement, lower standardized test scores, and increased mind wandering. They are more prone to suffer from PTS, anxiety disorders, and substance abuse. Some data suggest that low working memory capacity causes people to exhibit prejudicial behavior toward those who are different and for whom they have formed a dislike. Simply put, they are more intolerant, which is a recipe for disaster as we try to persuade people in foreign lands to become allies.

A study of 31 Marines carried out by Amishi Jha and her research team investigated whether mindfulness training would help troops maintain working memory under predeployment stress. The results suggest positive benefits for the Marines' operational effectiveness. The Marines who stuck with the training in a significant way "maintained the same perceived stress level and preserved or even improved their working memory capacity over their initial baseline." The Marines who didn't participate in a meaningful way had an increase in perceived stress and a diminished capacity for working memory. If these early results prove to be accurate over the long term, it could have significant positive implications for reducing battlefield errors and harm to noncombatants, and for improving the psychological health of our returning troops. It can give them a fair opportunity to get back to a normal life with the least amount of pain for them and their families.

⌒

One person who has been inspired by mental fitness training is Major General Walter Piatt, who has served 36 years in the U.S. Army. General Piatt has deployed four times since September 11, 2001. He served two tours in Afghanistan and two in Iraq. He recently served as commander of the U.S. Army Infantry School at Fort Benning in Georgia, the Army's premier training facility, before being chosen to lead the 10th Mountain Division at Fort Drum in Jefferson, New York. When I first met Walt, he was a colonel and has since been promoted. At that time, he shared with me his enthusiasm for the effects that mindfulness-based training could have on soldiers' readiness and their ability to return to civilian life.

General Piatt told me that when he first heard about mind fitness training, "I was convinced about the validity of what they were saying concerning how mental fitness could be sharpened, because what they said reflected the kinds of experiences I had in my last eight years. They simply nailed it."

Piatt was able to experience mindfulness training firsthand during the training of a group of 160 soldiers under his command at Schofield Barracks, Hawaii, who took part in a 2010 study on the effectiveness of mindfulness training in preparing soldiers to deploy. Piatt was very encouraged by what he heard and saw. "For one thing, soldiers started to see that mindfulness is not some abstract idea. It's a physical phenomenon that has to do with how they process and act on information. It's scientifically based, and it gave them practical skills that they could apply immediately in the field. They felt it was worth their time, and some people also said it helped bring their squad together, and squad cohesiveness is essential to combat effectiveness."

Piatt would like to see mental fitness become an essential element in predeployment training in the U.S. Army. "I would love to see this program emerge not as a specialty, a sideline," he says, "but as part of our entry-level training and part of the daily routine that we need to follow to create a resilient force. The Army is more receptive to such a program now, because of what we've been through and the complex environments we find ourselves in. We know we need to look at how we train the whole person, because we need the whole person in the kinds of conflicts we find ourselves in."

⌐⌐

Mylene Huynh was raised in Northern Virginia, the daughter of Vietnamese immigrants. Naturally, her ancestry can call to mind a very difficult time in America's recent history, so Mylene may have had some challenges growing up. If she did, you can't tell from her attitude and demeanor. Ever cheerful and with great military bearing, Mylene served for many years as a physician and a colonel in the U.S. Air Force and most recently as an integrative medicine consultant at Walter Reed National Military Medical Center. I first met her at a mindfulness and health conference. When I followed up with her in

Washington, she told me how she got started practicing mindfulness at the University of Virginia when she was premed. "College can be very stressful at times. I had by then heard about some of the scientific evidence of mindfulness's benefit." In college, she said, "I started practicing mindfulness meditation on a regular basis. I started to see things more clearly and found it very soothing. At the very least, it allows you to have some quiet, reflective time by yourself."

Even though she felt she "needed mindfulness more than ever during medical school," she dropped it because her other commitments were just too great. But after she graduated from medical school and began to practice medicine, she started to pick up mindfulness again because, she told me, "I started seeing so many patients who were suffering, and we have no easy treatments for them. Medications don't necessarily cure their pain. So many people have physical pain that results from life circumstances and how they react to them."

When Mylene was the medical operations squadron commander at Kirtland Air Force Base in Albuquerque, she began to collaborate with a radiologist, Dr. Lara Patriquin, who became interested in mindfulness because of the results she was seeing in studies of the brain. Together they introduced mindfulness to the medical staff. "What I had learned," Mylene said, "was that mindfulness practice helped me sustain the joy of medicine and avoid burnout. In primary care, you see patient after patient, and then you have administrative duties and demands from your superiors. You have limited time to sit with a patient, assess their symptoms, and make a diagnosis. I found mindfulness allows me to truly be present during my entire time with a patient, which helps me listen better, understand the patient's needs, and maintain my effectiveness as a caregiver."

In the initial program at Kirtland, about 30 participants took part, committing to an hour of practice at lunchtime once a week for six weeks. The response was very positive, and when Colonel Huynh was reassigned to Washington, Dr. Patriquin continued to work with a broad cross section of people on the airbase together with Major Corey Christopherson.

Like Liz Stanley and Walt Piatt, Mylene would like to see mindfulness-based practices more widely adopted as a way to build resiliency. "In the military, as in medicine, we tend to be very reactive," she says. "We want to treat something or fix a problem right away, with a silver bullet if need be. But mindfulness is not quite like that. It's not a sexy, glamorous, high-tech intervention, and it takes regular and steady application, but it works. And it contributes to good health and mental resiliency. Medicine should focus on *health*, not just *health care*. Health care alone may often come too late for our citizens and our service members. Health care tends to be a temporary bandage, whereas health is an ongoing state of well-being."

⌒

Mirabai Bush is in her 70s now, a very happy grandmother, yet she still exhibits the boundless energy and creative spirit of her youth, when she first started practicing mindfulness. One of the founders of the Center for Contemplative Mind in Society (first mentioned in Chapter 4), along with Daniel Goleman, Bush has been called "the grande dame of the movement to bring contemplative practices into the mainstream of society." Together with Goleman, she was instrumental in helping create Google's mindfulness and emotional intelligence course for its employees, called Search Inside Yourself. The program has been so successful that Google has been presenting it in its locations worldwide. I've had several delightful conversations with the Google employee who started it, Chade-Meng Tan, who has written *Search Inside Yourself,* a book that describes how the course benefits Google engineers, and how it can benefit people in any workplace.

Although in semiretirement, Mirabai Bush remains quite active in Contemplative Mind's initiatives, which include many programs to promote more mindful approaches to learning at the college level as well as a very successful program offering mindfulness practice to lawyers. In 2008, Bush and her colleagues were approached by Major Robert H. Williams, a U.S. Army chaplain who thought the center's experience in applied mindfulness might help with the rapidly increasing burnout rate among those who help soldiers deal with the pain, stress, and injury of military service. A report commissioned by the U.S. Army Surgeon General (published in 2005) found that 33 percent of behavioral health personnel and the "ministry teams" (which include chaplains) reported high or very high burnout. Physicians and other medical providers reported an even higher rate, at 37 percent.

In response to Major Williams's request, the center produced a review of literature about how mindfulness and related practices could help increase resiliency: "The Use of Meditation and Mindfulness Practices to Support Military Care Providers." The report became the basis for a landmark event in early 2009: a one-day symposium organized by the center that attracted a diverse group of 40 people, including representatives from many Army organizations, chaplains from various faith traditions, and mindfulness teachers and researchers. According to Mirabai:

> The people coming together in the room that day never thought they would find themselves sharing a day with some of the other people in the room—in the National Cathedral no less. Some people in the mindfulness world had been involved in anti-war activities and a lot of the military people thought that anyone who meditated was just too soft to make a serious decision. It turned out to be an amazing day. We found common ground in trying to help people who are suffering, and there were tears and laughter on all sides. In the process folks like me came to understand the needs and the worldview of those in the military, and they came to understand ours. I'm not sure what kind of programs will emerge from this dialogue, but we'll never think about people in the military in the same way again. We know their pain.

When we think of great wartime leaders, no one comes more readily to mind than Abraham Lincoln. No wartime president has had to endure what he had to—a war on our own soil, with our own citizens fighting each other—and he gave his own life for it. Lincoln never sought war, but he came to believe it was inevitable at the time. In his famous second inaugural address, inscribed along with the Gettysburg Address on the walls of the Lincoln Memorial, he made the point that neither side had wanted war.

With the end of the war only days away, the tone of the speech was sad: no doubt a reflection of his feelings about the tremendous loss of life and the destruction that had spread across the country. His final paragraph began, "With malice toward none, with charity toward all," one of the pithiest statements of a compassionate way of being ever uttered. That paragraph contains a series of goals including the line that became the motto for the U.S. Department of Veterans Affairs (then called the Veterans Administration), which is displayed on a pair of metal plaques flanking the entrance to the VA headquarters: "To care for him who shall have borne the battle and for his widow, and his orphan."

We need to do more to live up to that motto, and Anthony (Tony) King, Ph.D., may be able to help. A multifaceted neuroscientist, he's an assistant professor of psychiatry research at the University of Michigan, a member of the Trauma, Stress, and Anxiety Research Group, and a specialist in brain imaging; he also holds a master's degree in clinical psychology. Tony works with veterans at the VA Ann Arbor Healthcare System, where he has used a variety of techniques, including various mindfulness-based approaches, to help veterans suffering with post-traumatic stress. On the day I spoke with him, he had just finished an individual therapy session with a vet recently returned from Iraq.

"In working with vets," Tony told me, "I rarely talk about meditation or even mindfulness, since those words can seem abstract. I often say *grounding*. 'Let's try to be here now rather than someplace else.' So many of us are someplace else much of the time, obsessively plotting our future or rehashing an argument we had with a co-worker. For combat vets, when they're someplace else, they're taken back to the most horrific day that ever happened to them, more horrible than most people can imagine."

Tony is not only working with vets from Iraq and Afghanistan. "We're now seeing Vietnam vets who have never sought treatment. They worked their butts off their whole lives as a way to keep busy and avoid their thoughts and feelings about their trauma. Now that they are retiring or have to stop work for medical reasons, even after 40 years these thoughts and feelings are coming back up for them." King also confirmed for me something Walter Piatt had said. Not all veterans who experienced trauma end up with PTS. Some do not, and that's because, as Richie Davidson has often pointed out to me, humans are not one size fits all. We are capable of a broad range of responses.

Tony King and his colleagues carried out a pilot study of vets with PTS taking part in an 8-week mindfulness course that was adapted from a program for people with depression. He then worked with clinical psychologists and PTS specialists at the Ann Arbor VA to develop a new 16-week program specifically for combat PTS, combining mindfulness training, self-compassion exercises, and standard forms of PTS therapy in a group format for veterans returning from Iraq and Afghanistan. They are using before-and-after brain scans as well as traditional means of assessing PTS symptoms to study the effect of the mindfulness program. "When I went into this," he told me, "I wondered if doing meditation and yoga was going to be too weird and airy-fairy for the vets, but in fact, a lot of the vets seem to embrace things that we told them might seem a little flaky, like doing an awareness scan of every part of their body or very slowly and deliberately eating a raisin."

King carried out a study of 23 veterans of the wars in Iraq and Afghanistan, and the promising results of the study were published in 2016 in *Depression and Anxiety*, the official journal of the Anxiety and Depression Association of America. According to a University of Michigan Medical School summary of the findings, "Before the mindfulness training, when the veterans were resting quietly, their brains had extra activity in regions involved in responding to threats or other outside problems. This is a sign of that endless loop of hypervigilance often seen in PTSD. But after learning mindfulness, they developed stronger connections between two other brain networks: the one involved in our inner, sometimes meandering, thoughts, and the one involved in shifting and directing attention."

Some of the participants in King's studies have appreciated the fact that the practices did not focus on trauma but rather on daily life, enabling them to find less shaky emotional ground to walk on from moment to moment as they went through their day. What King calls mindful movement seems vitally important, since learning to be in the body is a very powerful way to return to the present moment. Physically oriented people like soldiers, firefighters, police, and other first responders often find movement-oriented therapies an easier place to start than those that deal primarily with thoughts.

When I met her, Emma Seppälä—now science director of Stanford University's Center for Compassion and Altruism Research and Education—was a young postdoctoral researcher at the Center for Healthy Minds, founded by Richie Davidson, doing preliminary research using yoga breathing as a primary means of care for combat vets with PTS. Richie told me he believes that body- and breathing-based practices may be most effective for PTS. In particular, some vets with trauma find it challenging to sit still for long periods and get highly anxious if asked to meditate. Breathing practice, on the other hand, can calm the autonomic nervous system within minutes, and the vets Davidson and Seppälä work with have responded very positively. The scientists' initial results indicate that after an eight-day breathing program, vets with PTS showed improved sleep, reduced anxiety, better memory, and reduced PTS. Rather than seeing the vets as victims, Emma is passionately committed to empowering returning vets with PTS. "Someone with the courage to go to war," she told me, "does not easily embrace victimhood. Here is an intervention that empowers vets instead of requiring dependence on a therapist or drug. My goal is for our research to shape policy and improve health care for veterans in the long run. It's gratifying to see them start to emerge as whole people again."

⌒

Our world got exponentially more complicated after 9/11. I, for one, believe that we could have turned that tragedy into our finest hour, without ending up in the entanglements we find ourselves in today. But, be that as it may, we did end up in two wars. Since then, our troops have once again shown a magnificent capacity for selflessness. They have sacrificed so much, tour after tour, because our country asked them. Their families have endured terrible heartache, anxiety, and loss.

We have an obligation, as policymakers and as citizens, to make sure we furnish our troops with everything they need to protect themselves. Time and time again, I've tried my best to be on the side of giving our troops everything they need to help them survive the war and come back home. And I have fought hard to make sure that when they return as veterans, they have the health care they need. Our military has among the most rigorous physical training in the world. We spend more for state-of-the-art weaponry than all the other countries in the world. Why is it that we haven't provided our troops with mind fitness training at the same level?

In delving into the research on mindfulness, I have found that it can be a potential force multiplier for our troops, and I have an obligation to pursue any and all opportunities to increase their physical and psychological health. It seems like common sense that teaching them to stay aware and connected to the present moment will benefit them in many ways. I'm glad that studies are starting to back this up so more people will understand the significance of mindfulness.

The people who serve in our military are putting their lives on the line on our behalf. They've committed themselves to doing what our leaders ask of them. Whatever our political views may be, we've all got to be deeply grateful for that. In return, let's make sure they get everything they need in order to do their jobs. And now more than ever, they need the mental fitness to deal with increasingly complicated situations. We have the physical training implemented, but that alone is not helping us reduce the numbers of psychological disorders. It alone has not lessened the burden of PTS. And it alone has not decreased the suicide rate. We must do more. And this means more studies of the benefits of mindfulness programs; less money spent on outdated weapons systems and more money spent on training for our troops; more training for our chaplains and medics to prevent burnout;

and stress reduction classes for the families who are left behind at home.

⌒

One of the most moving days I spent during the writing of this book was when I took a trip to the Gettysburg battlefield, a 90-minute drive north of Washington. It's the site of the bloodiest battle ever fought on American soil and the turning point of the Civil War. As I surveyed the ground of Pickett's Charge, like so many others before me, I felt the pain of brother fighting brother. For God's sake, nobody wants war, but war seems to happen. Until we find a way to end war, we had better try to conduct it in a way that decreases loss of life and damage all around.

From the site of Pickett's Charge, I made my way to the extreme north of the battlefield to Oak Hill and the Eternal Light Peace Memorial, dedicated by Franklin Delano Roosevelt and said to be the inspiration for Jacqueline Kennedy's request for an eternal light at JFK's grave. They had visited the monument together one lovely summer's day in 1962. Sadly, the peace memorial is rarely visited now. Too few get to take in its grandeur and its uplifting inscription: *Peace Eternal in a Nation United.*

At the end of my visit, I went to the cemetery that had been dedicated by President Lincoln, which created the occasion for one of the great documents of American history, the Gettysburg Address. It made me think that his message is not out of date. We need to learn from the harsh experiences of our modern-day wars as an expression of appreciation to those who fought and gave their lives. In our very day, we need to respond to the call of a President who knew the mental and physical toll of war on his soldiers, when he said that we need to be dedicated:

> . . . to the great task remaining before us—that from these honored dead we take increased devotion to that cause for which they gave the last full measure of devotion—that we here highly resolve that these dead shall not have died in vain—that this nation, under God, shall have a new birth of freedom.

WHAT YOU CAN DO

- Show a soldier or Marine the work that is already happening in the military to improve their performance and guard against PTS.

- Find out whether a local veterans hospital has a mindfulness program for returning veterans.

- Introduce mindfulness to a military family support group for those whose loved ones are away serving our country.

- Write your congressional representative or senator to encourage them to support mindfulness-based interventions for our troops.

CHAPTER 7

HOW MINDFULNESS CAN HELP US REDISCOVER OUR VALUES AND RESHAPE OUR ECONOMY

'Tis the gift to be simple. 'Tis the gift to be free
'Tis the gift to come down where we ought to be,
And when we find ourselves in the place just right,
'Twill be in the valley of love and delight.

— SHAKER SONG

At the peak of America's industrial revolution, my area of Ohio was booming. Youngstown was in the heart of the steel belt. Our region was referred to as the Steel Valley, and making steel and manufacturing heavy industrial products were, and are, in our blood. Many neighborhoods sprang up across from the steel mills that stretched for miles along the Mahoning River. One such neighborhood was Brier Hill. It was made up almost entirely of Italian families who came to the

United States to find work in the early part of the 20th century. They lived on this hill overlooking Youngstown Sheet and Tube so they could walk to work. From their front porches they could see the mill stacks spewing out fire, smoke, and God knows what else. The wives of the workers had to sweep soot from the mill off their porches at least once a day.

That soot was symbolic. It meant the family would be able to eat a good meal, make their rent payment, and possibly, if they were so blessed, buy their own home one day. It meant that they could afford to take their children to Idora Park, the old-time city amusement park on the other side of town. It meant that husbands and wives would have a couple of extra bucks to go see Tommy Dorsey or Glenn Miller when their traveling bands came through town. It meant, even if they had to keep sweeping the porch day after day, year after year, that their children could possibly work at Sheet and Tube or maybe, just maybe, go to college and become an engineer at the mill, or a doctor, or President of the United States. Family and friends lived close by in safe neighborhoods; gardens and chickens were raised in their backyards; residents were within walking distance of the butcher, the cobbler, the corner store, the church, the local park, and their favorite watering hole. They were connected. Not by texting or e-mail or social media, but through hugs, kisses, music, sips of wine, and laughter.

They were in America at a time of great optimism, and the sky—as dirty as it may have been—was the limit because Youngstown had the highest per capita income of any American city in the 1940s. While it may have been soot leaving the towering smokestacks in the valley, by the time it landed on the front porches of the homes on Brier Hill, it was gold dust.

⤳

As I think of Brier Hill, I'm struck by another challenge we face in our country: Can we recapture the kind of good life people had in a neighborhood like Brier Hill and yet do it in a 21st-century way—without the soot? Of course, I believe we can. Otherwise I would quit my day job.

I do think we can find the kind of new economy we need to keep people meaningfully employed, learn to live in better harmony with the earth, and be wiser in our use of resources and energy. Mindfulness is not the magic potion that gets us all that, but being more mindful can be a critical element in helping us along the way. In this book you've seen how mindfulness can help our schoolchildren and teachers; our health-care professionals and us, as their patients; and our troops, veterans, and others who serve us in uniform, whether putting out fires or responding to disasters. If more mindfulness makes its way into these aspects of our society, many citizens will lead a less stressful and more fulfilling life, and that alone is a good thing.

And yet, as I think of our schoolchildren educated in mindfulness as part of their curriculum, I have to ask myself what kind of livelihood and community and environment will they inherit. Will they live in a society that encourages connection and innovation or simply more consumerism? Are we going to give them a system that conserves resources and energy and cares for the earth? Are we going to give them livable communities where we walk and bike more and are able to enjoy nature close to where we live and work? A mindful nation is about much more than *just* making a living.

We spend one-third of our time working—when we are fortunate enough to have gainful employment. I can't say what jobs will be prevalent in the coming decades, but I do know that simply having a job will not be enough. We need to feel contentment, connection, and purpose. The workers up on Brier Hill felt a connection to their work. It was not always the easiest or cleanest job, but they understood how their steel was helping make America a strong country that could lead the world economically and politically. From the war years through the middle of the last century, they felt their work was a part of a larger national effort. They aspired to have their community prosper, and that is the heart of any successful economy.

These families made a comfortable living as a part of America's celebrated middle class, and yet they were part of a larger effort that enlisted all Americans. That was the American spirit that John F. Kennedy was calling forth in his famous statement, "Ask not what your country can do for you. Ask what you can do for your country." The mentality that came out of two World Wars and a Depression in between—that you were your brother's and sister's keeper—was seared into their psyche and carried over into postwar America. They stayed connected as a workforce in an attempt to protect workers from being treated unjustly and to increase opportunity for other workers to get in on the prosperity. They voted and were involved in the political process. They supported wise public investments that improved the quality of their communities. They were connected to the social infrastructure of their communities and supported police and school levies in order to strengthen them. They empowered their children's teachers and emphasized the value of education in all its forms. They volunteered at their churches and church festivals, for Boy Scout and Brownies troops, for the PTA, and at local charities. They understood their connection to the whole. This was their life, constantly being enriched by the lives of those around them.

I believe a lot of the anxiety we feel today is because our busyness and our overuse of technology disconnect us from each other. When you glance around a crowded restaurant, you will usually see two people sitting at a table facing each other, each looking at their own smartphone. Too often we are together but not necessarily connected. The disconnection can leave us feeling worn out, on edge, and scattered. At times it seems there isn't even room to take a deep breath. We feel anxiety if a text message isn't returned immediately. We get upset if someone is not instantly available for us. These are modern anxieties, self-imposed.

Mindfulness can help us reduce stress and raise our energy level. And one obvious place to start is in the workplace. Chade-Meng Tan started the mindfulness and social intelligence program at Google that I mentioned in the last chapter because he has the conviction that weaving this into our work gives us the best possibility of weaving it into our lives. We have gyms at or near our work to promote physical exercise, he says. In the same way, workplace facilities and programs for training the mind may someday become just as common. Ten minutes of mindfulness in the middle of a busy schedule may seem like a very small thing, but it can make a big difference.

Janice Marturano, whom I've had the pleasure of meeting and talking to on several occasions, taught mindfulness to many corporate leaders from around the world during her years as deputy general counsel for General Mills. She knows the tremendous positive impact mindfulness can have on the effectiveness of corporate leaders whose actions direct vast material and human resources. Janice, author of *Finding the Space to Lead*, founded the Institute for Mindful Leadership in 2011 because the requests to teach leaders and potential leaders became too great to do on a part-time basis. When he was chief information officer at Genentech, Todd Pierce collaborated with mindfulness teacher and executive coach Pamela Weiss of Appropriate Response to create an innovative mindfulness program for his department. More than 500 people took part in the Personal Excellence Program they developed, and the department went from being the lowest in job satisfaction to number two in the company. In 2015, *New York Times* reporter David Gelles published *Mindful Work: How Meditation Is Changing Business from the Inside Out*, documenting the rise of mindfulness-based programs in businesses across the country.

These programs do more than just increase workers' well-being on the job. They also enable them to work better in teams and make the critical, innovative decisions that will help our nation respond to the economic challenges of a fast-changing global economy. In light of this evidence, isn't it clear that we need to make more time for mindfulness in our workplaces?

⌒

In order to thrive, we *must* change. Neuroplasticity, which was discussed in Chapter 3, brings us the good news that *we can change* the pathways within our brains and do things differently. As easily as our brain developed to know how to ride a horse or plow a field, it changed and learned how to drive a car or run an open-hearth furnace. Immigrants who came to America had a shift in their brains when they went from thinking they could stay in their homeland to thinking they needed to go to America in order to reach their full potential. When they started to think about going to America, their brains began creating new neural pathways that planned out how they could get here, how they would find the money, and where they would go once they arrived. They literally changed their minds.

As a country of immigrants, innovators, and risk takers, we understand how to adapt to change and find the edge. Now we need to change our collective neuropathways and create a new dynamic in America. We need to join together and update our economic and governmental systems. The industrial model, which has resulted in large, overly bureaucratic organizations that don't communicate well with each other and lose touch with events on the ground, is an outdated method for organizing and governing our society. We need new ways of thinking and new ways of mobilizing ourselves. We need to reinvest in the people of our country so we can tap into their deep capacity for innovation to help us craft a new model to organize our society. We need systems that support our citizens to creatively participate in helping us meet these challenges. We may not know today precisely what ideas will positively transform the way we live, but mindfulness will help us see the best in the emerging ideas in our rapidly changing time.

And make no mistake about it, big challenges lie ahead. We need to research and develop the next genera-tion of energy and reduce our dependency on foreign oil. We need to live in better and deeper harmony with the earth. We need to transform our food system from one where a pound of food travels, on average, 2,000 miles, to one where we access more of our produce locally. We need to figure out how every citizen can get a quality education and adequate, affordable health care. We need to redesign our transportation systems and buildings to use a lot less energy. We need to reorganize our cities so they are denser, are filled with parks and gardens, and offer more ways to get around. We need to invest in the visual arts, performing arts, and martial arts. Mindfulness alone will not make this happen, but it will allow us to tap into the potential of every citizen and marshal all of the talents of this great country. A mindful nation is more able to change course and cut a new path when circumstances require it.

Seeing things clearly will also show us that there are still big hurdles for people of color in our economy. Even if jobs are being created, institutions are still biased. My hope is that increasing our awareness will help us see this and have the courage to change it.

I attended a program recently in which we combined reports and discussions on our thorny economic, environmental, and energy problems with times of quiet reflection and mindfulness. It makes for a good combination. The program was led by Jonathan Rose, co-founder of the Garrison Institute and a leading affordable housing developer and innovative philanthropist. Tall and strong with a salt-and-pepper beard, he comes across as a gentle soul with a deep, strategic mind. Under his direction, Garrison has been sponsoring conferences like the one I attended, titled "Climate, Cities, and Behavior," inviting a select group of cognitive and behavioral researchers, real-estate developers, corporate leaders, government agency heads, and environmental-action innovators from all across the country to participate. The program was supported by foundations seeking innovative approaches to climate change, covering the cost of the program's research and administration. Participants just needed to get themselves there; room and board was covered. Garrison is a magical place: a sprawling former Catholic monastery that sits on the palisades of the Hudson River across from West Point. Just walking onto the property, you relax and open up. I'm sure the monks felt it too.

A key question explored at these conferences is whether we can generate more pro-environmental and pro-social behaviors through better understanding of our innate cognitive makeup and how our brains function. Many people have worked hard to change environmental behaviors by trying to alter people's *attitudes* about the environment—with little success. It turns out that the mind is wired to work the other way around. It's much more effective to first shift behavior; attitudes will then follow. For example, if you coax people to recycle or insulate their homes, their attitudes toward environmental protection overall become stronger. For another example, think of how our grandparents originally felt about technology, the advance of computers and e-mail. For the most part, they thought all this new technology was confusing and probably bad for you, and that there was no chance they would ever use it. That is, until they realized that they could easily see new pictures of their grandchildren who lived far away from them. I've met many grandparents who are on e-mail now for that sole purpose, and many now are beginning to make video calls on Skype so they can interact with their family. This change in actions—in behavior—has changed their attitude toward technology. They are not only more amenable to it, but they are actually enjoying it. All the arguments in the world could not get them to love computers, but once they began to feel the benefits, suddenly their attitude changed.

Those who come to the Garrison environmental conferences—such as the green innovators Paul Hawken and Van Jones—are passionately interested in the mechanisms of human behavior. Jonathan Rose invites people with a strong interest in how our brain functions—such as Daniel Siegel, a prominent psychiatrist from UCLA—to present the latest understanding of the brain's enormous capacity to change and adapt. Part of this study involves understanding the brain habits, or *cognitive biases*, we employ to get through our day. For the most part, these brain habits are beneficial, but at times they can also work against our best interests. For example, we tend to favor the way things already are and will not change something unless circumstances require us to change. This *status-quo bias* makes us reliable and consistent, but it also means that if a programmable thermostat is installed in our home, very few of us are likely to change its settings. Realizing this, Jonathan approached someone he knew at the Home Depot Foundation to see whether the company would consider setting its programmable thermostats to an energy-efficient setting so that consumers (who most likely are not going to change the setting) would end up saving themselves money and reducing demand on our energy system. The good news is that Home Depot already had such a plan in the works. The company has almost 2,000 stores across the country. Imagine the savings.

At the time I met environmental innovator and chief product officer of the International WELL Building Institute Rachel Gutter, she was director of the Center for Green Schools at the U.S. Green Building Council. The center promotes the development of environmentally literate students so children learn from a young age about where the real source of our prosperity lies: the earth itself. Rachel's enthusiasm is contagious, and she's a believer in "how much value a few minutes of silence can be"—a few minutes of mindfulness of the world around you—when you're trying to foster creative thinking about how to make a better relationship with the earth. Rachel emphasized to me that green schools with green gardens save school districts money while offering great educational benefits. Green schools have systems that alert the students about when to turn off the lights or when to open the windows and shut off the air conditioning. Subjects like biology, chemistry, and math can be livened up when they are taught in the garden behind the school, the "edible schoolyard." Tending a garden teaches the children where broccoli and beans really come from, and it also teaches them that things grow and develop with proper effort and time. And hopefully they will become aware that with patience and effort they can grow too: emotionally, intellectually, and spiritually. They might also learn about the value of good, wholesome food. Not a bad thing at all, since several studies show that children who eat healthy foods during the course of a day are better behaved, able to pay more attention, and less likely to become obese.

Alice Kennedy, community liaison and strategic project manager with the Baltimore Neighborhood Energy Challenge, is a mindfulness practitioner who is also plugged into the Garrison network. She is a bright and energetic advocate for individuals' reducing their household energy usage. The Baltimore Neighborhood Energy Challenge, she told me, asks residents to volunteer their time to become "Energy Captains," trained in energy conservation and community organizing. "We build a network of residents who can talk about energy conservation on a level that resonates with their peers," Alice says. "We simply say, 'Try this,' making sure that what we suggest is something they would be open to doing. We listen and keep our ego out of the way."

Alice reminded me of another longtime activist, Pat Rosenthal from Youngstown. She was instrumental in the city's award-winning 2010 plan, which serves as a model to shrink cities to a more manageable and sustainable size. That work is now being carried forward with Global Green, an organization with 31 affiliates worldwide that seeks to bring about a shift in values and redefine a prosperous life—the good life—as one where we respect the earth and do not tax it beyond its capacity. That's mindful living.

And that kind of living appeals to people in America who may have political differences over many other matters. Certain values unite us. Rachel Gutter told me about a Tea Partier who has been one of the biggest advocates for green schools in Kentucky. In Kansas, Jeff Risley, a Republican who presented at Garrison, spoke about the Take Charge Challenge, which created a friendly competition among six Kansas communities to see who could reduce energy consumption by the greatest percentage, resulting in 7 million kilowatt hours per year in reduced consumption. Over 10,000 people attended events because, Risley believes, he promoted the program by appealing to values such as stewardship, community, thrift, independence, and pragmatism. These values resonate in the heartland.

As we've seen, mindful approaches are attracting a lot of attention in education, health care, and the military. The economy, environment, energy: these are new frontiers for mindful approaches but no less important, in my view. It may seem like these little programs here and there are mere pebbles measured against the daunting challenges we face. And yet lots of little things here and there can lead to systemic change. As I noted in the introduction, the age of oil—which has shaped our current economy and our energy network while delivering us our most pressing environmental challenges—began as little things here and there, and before we knew it, a whole new system was born. The same can happen again with the innovative approaches that are coming out of the intellectual wells of our nation.

⌒

Thermostats. Energy challenges. Turning off the lights. Sustainability. No surprise that we've been hearing these words and phrases a lot in the past few years. One of the most pressing challenges for us to tackle is how our country generates, stores, and transmits energy. It took billions of years for all the carbon-based fuels like coal and oil to get into the earth. In just over 100 years, we will have removed it and burned it all. I am no scientist, but it seems to me that this will have some negative effect on our atmosphere. Not only that, but when fossil fuels are depleted, where will our next energy sources come from? We need to be very direct in asserting that 98 percent of scientists are saying that our behavior has the planet warming at a pace that could be very destructive if we don't reverse current trends.

What does *mindfulness* have to do with energy? For one thing, by increasing our awareness of our daily habits, mindfulness can make us more attentive to not wasting energy. Also, as I learned from the environmental activist Paul Hawken, it can help us be honest about where we are as a society, the challenges we face, and what we need to do. Paul founded the garden tool company Smith & Hawken and the solar technology company OneSun, so he has an entrepreneurial mind, which he has tried to bring to bear on the realities of our energy system and our need to live in better relationship with the earth. Hundreds of groups doing that kind of work were documented in Paul's book *Blessed Unrest: How the Largest Social Movement in History Is Restoring Grace, Justice, and Beauty to the World*. Many more have sprung up since the book came out several years ago.

During one lengthy conversation with me, he pointed out that a major shift has recently happened that profoundly affects our ability to do things in the same old way. Until 1974, oil had been steady at $16 a barrel in 2010 dollars. After that it started rising rapidly, and for a long time it hovered above $100 a barrel. Although it has dropped recently, it will inevitably head back up as we have to go to more and more expensive means of extraction. Commodity prices for metals and agricultural feedstocks have similarly shifted. Iron, copper, and all the other metals that are needed to make an industrial society work, as well as corn, decreased in price for 150 years by an average of 1.2 percent a year. In the decade after 2002, however, *all the savings accrued over those 150 years of price decreases were erased*. China and India, with more than a billion people each and experiencing rapid industrialization, have aggressively mined a lot of the commodities on earth. *We cannot live the way we've lived before.*

We send $1 billion a day out of the United States, primarily through the gas pump, to buy oil from countries that are often hostile toward us. Some of them take a portion of these petrodollars and fund global terrorist organizations. We have been involved in two wars—which are in substantial measure about fighting for resources—for more than a decade, and fighting still rages on. The cost of these wars will be in the trillions, not to mention the lives lost and injuries suffered. And the money being spent has been borrowed. The bill will be sent to our children and grandchildren.

⌐⌐

What if we all became conservationists? Let's conserve our energy and stop spending so much money in a way that leads to little benefit at home. Perhaps some of this wealth can make its way into the hands of entrepreneurs, both private and public, who will re-create our urban cores, renovate our historic town squares and theaters, build bike trails, spruce up our parks, and provide seed money for our urban farms. What if that money were used to provide incentives to businesses and workers for telecommuting? Imagine if it went to connecting our country via high-speed rail and brought elegance and comfort back to travel. Imagine how many of our laid-off building-trades members could go back to work to build the high-speed rail lines, or how many steelworkers would be needed to make the steel for the railcars. Think of how many of our sons and daughters could start companies or work for companies creating a new energy economy. We need a new energy system that respects and honors the basic American value of frugality. Conservation means jobs for those people who create the systems that conserve. When I asked him how a new energy economy can create jobs, Paul Hawken replied, "By plugging the holes and closing the loops."

A key part of the American way of life is an entrepreneurial spirit, and people like Paul Hawken, who has lots of experience as a businessman, know that without involvement from business, no transformational program will get off the ground. As I've said earlier, we need every sector of American society pulling in the same direction.

Hawken recently eulogized Ray Anderson, the late CEO of a carpet manufacturing company, Interface, who became a well-known environmental innovator. Hawken said of Anderson: "For Ray, no longer were there human systems and ecosystems. They were one system, and he understood that the laws of physics and biology prevailed."

Another leading whole-systems thinker whom I've had the pleasure to meet is Peter Senge, author of *The Fifth Discipline: The Art and Practice of the Learning Organization*. His work has been applied in every business sector in this and many other countries. He helps corporate leaders see the interconnectedness in the systems they work within. In *The Necessary Revolution: How Individuals and Organizations Are Working Together to Create a Sustainable World*, he describes the Coca-Cola integrated water management plan, in which Coke signed a five-year partnership with the World Wildlife Fund that would help Coke better manage its water usage. Then CEO and chairman Neville Isdell said, "We should not cause more water to be removed from a watershed than we replenish."

Senge offers plenty of other examples of "plugging the holes and closing the loops." In Sweden, for example, local businesses work together to reduce their energy costs in what are called "green zones." In one case, a McDonald's, a gas station, and a car dealership designed an interconnected energy system. The excess heat from the restaurant kitchen is piped directly to heat the car dealership and the filling station. And overall energy use was cut by 80 percent. That's the kind of conservation we need.

⌒

My interest in finding moments of simplicity and a deeper connection to the outdoors has taken me to some unexpected places. One of my favorite memories is sitting with a few other people under a tree in the pitch dark, at about 5 A.M. in northern Ohio. The forest was silent except for an infrequent rustle of the leaves beneath me or my camouflage jacket scraping against the tree bark. We sat for a while as light slowly crept across the sky. Then, as if organized and planned, the forest woke up. Birds slowly began to chirp. One by one, turkeys fell from the trees. My heart raced as I tried to stay calm, but I couldn't. My first turkey hunt was one of the most exhilarating experiences of my life. Sitting silently in the wild gave me a new perspective on life and a new appreciation of why millions of Americans love to hunt.

As the symphony of sounds reached a crescendo, it occurred to me that all Americans, no matter what their politics, would be amazed and awed by what I had experienced. Avid hunters and sportsmen obviously feel that wonder or they would not be so passionate about the lifestyle. And any member of the Sierra Club or Environmental Defense Fund would likely say that deep and direct experiences of nature like the one I was having made them advocate for a clean environment. An appreciation of nature and our environment cuts across party lines and can unite us.

Like most new hunters, I had some reservations about hunting an animal. I recalled a story my grandmother told of how as a Depression-era teen she had to "process" the chickens from her family's backyard coop. She had to take life in order for her and her five siblings to have a filling meal. Her experience may be why we said grace before every meal. We were taught to be thankful for our blessings and for all those who made the sacrifices that enabled us to eat. I also realized that for thousands of years humans have been hunting in order to stay alive. And in most of these instances the animals were honored as life-giving beings. Animals supported and promoted the life of our species. In many ancient myths they were deified. Hunting for food seemed a lot more humane than some of the disturbing and unhealthy processes used by big agriculture today.

If I told you of a group that had the motto "Conservation today, wetlands for tomorrow," who would you think it was? Would you guess that this conservation group, with 700,000 members, started because of a concern that the rapid loss of wetlands would destroy the habitat for waterfowl? Or that this group has, since its inception more than 80 years ago, conserved more than 14 million acres of waterfowl habitat in North America? Would it have to be a leftist environmental group that understands the importance of wetlands to a habitat or a group that is funded by progressive activists from New York and Los Angeles?

Not so. It's Ducks Unlimited, a group primarily made up of hunters and sportsmen and women from small towns all over the world. These members understand the value of our environment. They support, through volunteer hours and donated money, the hard and tedious work of protecting our sensitive habitat. While collectively we seem to be letting our environment deteriorate willy-nilly, that doesn't reflect what most people tell me about their appreciation of the earth. They don't really want to see all our forests bulldozed to make way for parking lots and malls. Down deep, most of us see our environment as something to be treasured. Most of us carry some sense of responsibility to be stewards of God's earth. Most of us want to assure our children and grandchildren a safe and healthy planet.

For me, sitting under that tree while turkey hunting felt similar to sitting down while practicing mindfulness. I was sitting in awareness, taking in all the sounds and sights, and feeling the beauty of the connectedness of life in the wild. Watching the turkeys look for food or a mate, I thought of how absurd it would be for that turkey to knowingly destroy its own environment. Our species—as grand as it is—appears to be the only one that destroys its own habitat willingly, and also one of the few that gangs up on other members of the species to fight them. But we don't have to.

Sitting there, I thought of the ritual of going hunting with your friends—the campfire and cooking the night before, getting up early and being together without talking. A routine like that connects us to each other. Imagine a world where we all took a few moments and sat to watch what we were doing in our own environment. And imagine if we could read the signs of what's going on with the natural world in the intuitive and honest way that the old-time farmers and fisherfolk did.

We would see that digging into the planet for energy at all costs to support our lifestyles is gambling with our children's lives. We would see that cutting down vast swaths of rainforest, ruining communities in the process, and tampering with the atmospheric balance is reckless, even mindless. We would see that the earth needs stewardship, oversight, and regulation. We would see through the barrage of television advertising that tries to persuade us that our food is straight from the family farm or that a few green statements amount to a real energy policy. And yet, in that quiet, we would also see that anger, bitterness, and dark, depressive thoughts do us no good. We will not motivate ourselves or others through fear and shame.

The web of life is complex. It's hard to sort out how it all works, much less solve all the problems it throws up as we try to get by on our little planet. There are no easy answers, but I do have the conviction that mindfulness can help nurture the innovative thinking required to find the emerging solutions we need. We all can take a few minutes each day to just stop, breathe, and watch. If we do, we may come to feel that the economic, environmental, and energy systems we live under now—in spite of all the conveniences and benefits they have brought us over years—need to be revolutionized. We still have a good life. Let's work to keep it that way.

What You Can Do

- Find out if anyone in your workplace is interested in a mindfulness class or group. See if starting and ending meetings with quiet time and reflective time can make a difference. Some groups find it makes the discussions better paced and more respectful.

- Get involved with local groups working to create a new, sustainable vision for your neighborhood.

- Join an organization that advocates sustainability in the area that excites you most.

- If you are in an older city that has lost population, organize a group to develop a plan to right-size your city.

- Support active transportation (walking and biking instead of using powered transportation) as a great way to practice some mindfulness on the go. Join a transportation advocacy group that supports high-speed rail, bike trails, and urban parks. Encourage your local elected officials to create places that encourage us to slow down and pay attention: open spaces and parks, urban gardens, farmers' markets. If you have a farmers' market, go there. Is there a mindfulness information booth there?

CHAPTER 8

HOW MINDFULNESS CAN HELP US HELP OURSELVES AND OUR COUNTRY

*What we need in the United States is not division;
what we need in the United States is not hatred . . . but
love and wisdom, and compassion toward one another.*

— ROBERT F. KENNEDY

November 6, 2004, was one of the toughest days of my life. The hospital called my mother a little after midnight to tell her that my grandfather's condition had worsened. She phoned me and then picked me up at my house a few minutes later. We rushed to the hospital fearing the worst. We walked into the hospital room, saw him lying in bed, and realized he was already gone. I stared at his body in disbelief and then turned to look at my grandmother, wondering what she was feeling. Her partner of more than 60 years, a giant of a man who had stood by us all, would no longer be there for her or any of us. I was devastated.

A few days later we held the wake and the burial Mass. I can only remember a few things from that time. The first is when they were preparing to close the casket. I couldn't stop crying and saying, "I love you, Grandpa!" Something else I remember vividly is the sermon given by my confirmation sponsor and one of my dearest friends, Father Ron Nuzzi of the University of Notre Dame. His theme for the eulogy was that Grandpa had "the strength to be gentle." He said Grandpa was a true gentleman, a *gentle* man. Truly strong men are gentle, he said. I have always felt that my grandfather embodied what we love and admire most in people: kindness, generosity, warmth, compassion, and loyalty to family, church, community, and country. He was not ashamed to be gentle, and he never pretended to be somebody he was not. He was kind and gentle, period. He was okay with that, and so were we.

I see in my grandfather an example for our country. Consider where bravado and ego-based posturing have put us during the past several decades. It has cost us too many lives, as well as a lot of money. America has always been strongest when we have been tough but gentle. Gentleness is not a sign of weakness; it's a sign of strength. We all know from the playground that the one who is acting the toughest is really the most insecure. America is at its best when we are confident. I am sorry to say that we have lost our footing. We are running around now in different directions, looking over our shoulder, scared and unsure. We don't know what to do or when to do it. If we could just slow down a bit, perhaps we'd see the answer.

My grandfather was my hero, an immediate personal inspiration. To me, heroes are people who overcome great odds to achieve great things, who have sacrificed their own lives in order to save others, and who have stared fear in the eye and overcome it. We build memorials to honor them individually and to celebrate the heroic traits they embody. Heroic qualities rest latent within each of us, only waiting to be brought to life. We love heroes, and we need them too.

Throughout our conversation in this book, I've introduced you to people I've met who are the kind of heroes we need. They're doing some of the most advanced research, clinical application, and on-the-ground implementation of mindfulness and related practices in America. They're pioneers who are helping us gain a deeper understanding of what it means to be a human being and what a miraculous reservoir of ability we can draw on to deal with the challenges of being alive in the 21st century. A revolutionary step like the Apollo moon shot required a centralized government program. Right now the mindfulness revolution is an organic, grassroots movement. In order for it to infuse all aspects of our society, its research and implementation should have the helping hand of government.

What we are talking about here is a growing personal and communal journey that can help us bring out our country's best. It's a way to increase our awareness of what's important to us, and what our priorities are, both as individuals and as a nation. This journey takes great courage, but the people whose stories I've shared let us know that all human beings are going through these same difficulties and challenges. More important, they let us know that all of us—Marines, firefighters, parents, students, environmental advocates, business leaders, health-care workers, hospital patients, veterans, and others—have the innate ability to change our minds.

And there are many more heroes out there doing mindfulness work in this country, changing lives, and reversing negative trends and creating positive ones. I'd like to mention a few more who are particularly close to my heart because they are working with people with addiction and mental health issues, young people, and expectant parents, and by doing so are building social capital—the economic value that results from taking care of one another and working together to create a healthier society.

As co-chair of the Congressional Addiction, Treatment and Recovery Caucus, I've had the opportunity to learn just how much damage addiction is doing to American communities. The opiate epidemic over the past few years has torn the heart out of so many communities. In 2016, we lost more citizens to overdose deaths related to opiates than we did during the entire Vietnam War. Yes, the entire war versus one year of overdoses. This is overwhelming our treatment and rehabilitation systems, burning out our first responders, and sucking already limited resources from our local governments. Ohio, New Hampshire, West Virginia, and Kentucky are some of the hardest hit states. Many of the best treatment facilities are using mindfulness-based programs and seeing promising results in preventing relapse, including Mindfulness-Based Relapse Prevention, founded by the late Alan Marlatt and now under the direction of his protégée Sarah Bowen. And mindfulness is also making important inroads in the treatment of many mental health concerns, from depression to social anxiety to obsessive-compulsive disorder, especially in North America through the work of Zindel Segal, one of the founders of Mindfulness-Based Cognitive Therapy (MBCT), and his many colleagues training people in and researching MBCT.

Nancy Bardacke, a longtime midwife and grand-mother, is the founder of the Mindfulness-Based Childbirth and Parenting Program (MBCP) and author of the bestseller *Mindful Birthing*. Nancy recognizes how stressful pregnancy, childbirth, and early parenting can be. She has found that the expectant parents who learn mindfulness through her program develop skills for working with the stresses of pregnancy and everyday life. They can more effectively cope with the pain and fear of childbirth and the stresses of parenting. Preliminary evidence is showing that mindfulness practice helps the mother deal with all the stresses that come with having and caring for a baby. The skills Nancy teaches can be utilized throughout the process of raising the child and "can interrupt intergenerational patterns of dysfunction" like shaken-baby syndrome. Parents who take MBCP classes give birth to their babies around the same time and often remain in contact afterward, forming little communities to support each other. Keeping connected to such a community, Nancy says, is one of the healthiest things parents can do for themselves and their children.

Gina Biegel, a young licensed marriage and family therapist with boundless energy and inspiration, is doing great work in the area of teen stress reduction, in a program she calls Stressed Teens. She has adapted MBSR for teens and is arming them with the skills they need to keep themselves balanced in a world that can be difficult and complicated. She has worked a lot with teens who have mental health difficulties, and has also done some work with teens with cancer. When teenagers find a deep resilience, and even cheerfulness, in the midst of terrible circumstances, they demonstrate the small-h heroism we are all capable of.

Vinny Ferraro and Chris McKenna at the Mind Body Awareness Project (MBA) in Oakland, California, are two tough dudes bringing mindfulness to youth in a postindustrial city with a high rate of gang activity. Don't let the tattoos fool you; they are savvy professionals in social service. They work in juvenile halls, detention camps, and at-risk schools in California, serving young people with histories of violence, substance abuse, and deep trauma. I visited these guys in Oakland during one of their training sessions for counselors. They have an impressive ability to cut through the rhetoric and gamesmanship that young adults (and all of us, at times) put forward. As Vinny says, they get "super-duper real" with the kids. Through mindfulness techniques, the MBA counselors are able to let 12- and 13-year-olds see for the first time that it's okay to be who they are and that they don't have to belong to a gang to attain self-fulfillment. One child in "juvie," hardened by all the deaths of friends and family to drugs and violence, hid behind a rock-hard exterior. In a group session with a counselor, she simply let him talk, and then allowed a long silence during which the counselor began to cry, and the young boy himself began to cry, prompting an older boy in the group to say, "It's okay. Men cry."[4]

The brothers Atman and Ali Smith, along with Andres Gonzalez, run the Holistic Life Foundation in Baltimore, Maryland, which they founded 16 years ago after they all graduated from the University of Maryland and decided to return to their neighborhood and do what they could to help. I visited with the Baltimore Boys, as I now call them, to learn about all they do with the young children in their city. They connect with the most at-risk kids through hip-hop while simultaneously integrating yoga and urban gardening into the kids' lives. The kids are changing before their very eyes, and Baltimore is a better city because of the foundation's work.

Yoga helped me synchronize my mind and body and build resiliency when I was younger. So seeing these kids sitting on yoga mats practicing mindfulness, I immediately wanted to replicate the program in cities across the nation. The Baltimore Boys are streetwise, and they live where they work. They've done the work for years while short on resources but long on love. Johns Hopkins did a preliminary study that suggested that the work they're doing had a positive impact on problematic responses to stress—including rumination (continually thinking about the same thing), emotional arousal (being overly reactive emotionally), and intrusive thoughts (having thought patterns that create ongoing anxiety). The university is now funding a larger-scale study of the program. It's been nice to see organizations and philanthropists locally and nationally stepping up to get behind their work.

These people and many others all over America and the world are changing the way we approach chronic poverty and disconnection. These programs reveal to our children that a negative and dangerous life is not their only option. With mindfulness skills they see that they have choices and the wherewithal to overcome the adversity in their lives. These programs can grow and lead to deep, systemic change, which is exactly what we need to help the many people living in poverty. If we can reorganize this system, our country will be a safer and healthier place because of it.

⌒

In this book we've seen people who have created classrooms that teach kids how to mobilize their power of attention and direct it toward schoolwork. They teach kids how to cultivate compassion and implement kindness in their daily lives. We've seen how our friends and family can reduce their own stress levels and how this can help the body do what is natural: heal itself. We've seen how health-care workers and others who serve the public can use mindfulness to guard against burnout. We've seen how military service members and veterans can benefit from improving brain function to handle the ferocity of war. As I've said, mindfulness is not a silver bullet, but it can help us better negotiate the complexity of life today.

In a mindful nation, we will still misplace our keys. We will still forget people's names. We will still say and do things that may hurt others, including those we love. We will say the exact wrong thing at exactly the wrong time. But in each of these instances, with mindfulness, we may do it just a bit less. We may see the humor in our mistakes and be able to laugh at ourselves more. We may be just a little less critical of others, and of ourselves. Or we may deal with our mistakes more quickly and with a more sincere and kind heart. We may more easily forgive the people who have hurt us. We may sit down and have civil political conversations with those who strongly disagree with us. My goal is not that America will become a perfect nation. My goal is that America will be a kinder, more compassionate nation, because I know down deep in my heart that we are a kinder, more compassionate country than is evident today. Reviving our compassionate spirit will allow us to listen carefully to each other, find points of agreement, and recapture the unity of purpose that made America great.

A mindful nation is about recognizing that we are all connected: we are in this together. At present, we feel divided and scared, and have been made to believe that independence means we are totally on our own. But our experiences—as individuals and as a country—tell a different story. We know that when we join together, work together, and care about each other, our freedom actually increases. Real independence emerges when we know how to support each other. The Declaration of Independence was a communal act.

When Karen Armstrong, the great religious scholar, is asked what unites all our major faiths, she responds, "Compassion." Our evolutionary psychologists tell us the same. And Charles Darwin, the man often misquoted to justify the brutality of capitalism, wrote, "Those communities which included the greatest number of the most sympathetic [i.e., empathetic] members, would flourish."

The every-man-for-himself model cuts against what all of our great religions have taught us; it also goes against what our great scientists are teaching us, and it denies what we know in our hearts. It's time for compassion to come front and center in our public discourse. We need to get away from worshipping at the altar of profit and markets as if they were flawless deities. If we care about each other, invest in each other, and put the well-being of human beings first, we will soften the rough edges of the market system and all of us will profit more.

Mindfulness can help us slow down enough, and pay attention enough, to see clearly the basic human truth Darwin stated. We're not going to get this from the business talk shows: they tell us that if we buy the right stock, we'll flourish. We won't get it from the news channels: they tell us that if we have a certain political view and vote the right people into office, we will flourish as never before. We won't get it from the commercials telling us that the latest product will bring us deep satisfaction. We'll get it by slowing down and seeing how powerful compassion can be.

In our own lives, we can remember a parent or teacher or coach who cared about us, who was the reason we were able to go beyond ourselves and perhaps achieve great things. Their compassion helped us flourish. We know, especially in times of overwhelming grief, what a compassionate friend can mean. Such caring is life giving, and our country can use some of that right now. For us, creating a mindful nation requires us to recognize that compassion can be the foundation of recapturing the American spirit. The next great re-creation of America is not going to come from how much our government spends. The question must be: Do our investments sustain or create systems that are compassionate or simply create wealth at any cost? People across the political spectrum need to honestly consider this. A person trapped in a hopeless welfare system or poor educational system is not being treated compassionately, nor is a business that is completely reliant on government subsidies or the continued growth of the military-industrial complex.

A mindful nation debates these issues with the goal of creating opportunity for all our citizens in a sustainable nation. Debate—which was invented as a means to find the truth and the best way forward rather than to polarize—should sharpen these points and help each side see its perspective in a new way. And as we've discussed, mindfulness helps everyone involved care about each other, which provides the basis for us to work on these tough problems together. We thereby have a good shot at not just surviving, but thriving. If he were here today, I believe Charles Darwin would support the work of first-class centers of scientific research like Stanford and Emory in studying how we can cultivate compassion.

⌒

One of my favorite lines from the *Art of War* by Sun Tzu, an ancient manual for dealing effectively with conflict in war, business, and life, is "Attain both hard and soft." To me, this means that in any given moment we need the ability to be simultaneously firm and gentle. This can be challenging, but Martin Luther King, Jr. offered us an example of holding hard and soft together. He pointed out that love without power is ineffectual, and power without love is destructive.

When human beings combine these qualities, they're drawing on their innate mindfulness, awareness, and kindness. And neuroscience is starting to prove that all of these can be cultivated in greater measure, giving us an increased capability to approach our problems and challenges with nuance and awareness of the whole picture, the perspectives of other people, and the unfolding patterns that allow us to be insightful about dangers and opportunities that lie ahead—what the innovative thinker Thomas Homer-Dixon calls "prospective mind." In this way, we can help reestablish our collective mindfulness and regain our sense of balance, which is what it means to be resilient. We can't determine exactly what the future will be, what tomorrow will bring, or even what the next moment will bring, but we can determine how we will be in our body and mind, whatever may come.

Mindfulness helps us to be prepared for whatever comes our way. John Wooden, the legendary basketball coach at UCLA, used to shock his players with his opening lesson. He gathered them in the locker room before the first practice, not for a pep talk or a presentation on defensive strategy or ball-handling skills. He taught them how to put on their socks. If you don't put on your socks properly, he explained, you get a wrinkle, and when you have a wrinkle, it causes a blister, and when you have a blister, you can't run and jump properly, and so on. Paying attention to that simple act of pulling up your socks is mindfulness. If we take our time with the small things, the big things will come along.

A bumper sticker on my office wall says, "Celebrate Fiercely." That's what a mindful nation does. We celebrate the amazing journey of our country. The ups and downs. The tragedies and triumphs. I wrote this book to celebrate the talent and compassion of the people helping others to cultivate their innate mindfulness in so many different spheres. They've seen people change before their very eyes. They've seen members of the military become more resilient so they have a better chance of fully reconnecting with their loved ones when they come back from war. They have seen veterans let go of years of pain and suffering, they have seen young kids become more attentive and caring students, and they have seen people suffer less because of a health problem. We need to celebrate this work. Today. Now.

This work has just begun, and the interest in a more mindful nation keeps growing. Many of our citizens are realizing that going faster and faster to solve our problems has not worked, and neither has waiting for our outer circumstances to change on their own— through the invisible hand of the market or pure luck. We intuitively know that if we are going to recapture the American spirit, it will be because millions of our citizens will begin to see the power of being connected and moving in the same basic direction, regardless of our inevitable and necessary differences.

We know we're stronger when we're caring about each other and creating a future that works for us all. My grandparents' generation proved that. The magic of mindfulness in all of the stories told here is that the people involved care about each other and care for each other. The doctors with their patients, the teachers with their students, the community organizers with their neighbors. A sense of common purpose and love for one another makes it all work. Deep down most Americans want to be a part of something bigger than themselves, and the work in mindfulness is an opportunity to do that in every corner of this magnificent land of ours. And once people learn approaches to helping themselves and making their minds and bodies more resilient—learning to be there for themselves and others—they will inspire other people to do the same.

If you have a dollar bill in your pocket or purse, look at it: on the reverse side, directly under the pyramid, the phrase *Novus Ordo Seclorum* appears. It roughly translates as "A New Order of the Ages." The new order created by our American experiment was based on the principle that the people are responsible for making the country work. It's up to us. The values we need to shoulder this responsibility are self-reliance, hard work, and a commitment to a bright and prosperous future for our children. We can't predict their future, but we can help them be there fully when they get there—able to work creatively and with resilience no matter what they encounter.

We need to raise our children in a nation that teaches them to be mindful, that teaches them about the importance of kindness and being connected to their fellow human beings and the environment that sustains them. We need a nation that teaches them to appreciate their basic human goodness and see that goodness in others. I want that kind of country for my niece and nephews, for the Bellas and Masons and Bradys in my district, for all of us. And I will join with the heroes and pioneers I've talked about in this book to bring about that kind of world for us all. Together, we will continue to promote, encourage, and celebrate this important work. It's helping us all recapture the spirit of what it means to be an American. Join us.

To enable you to learn how straightforward mindfulness practice is, I have asked my friend Susan Bauer-Wu, whom we met in Chapter 3, to offer a simple description of mindfulness practice and a kindness practice in the afterword.

Following her very clear and simple instruction is a section that lists many resources you can draw from as you seek to apply mindfulness and related disciplines in your own life or the life of your community. I've included the organizations of all the people mentioned in this book, as well as many others. If you would like to see whether mindfulness or social and emotional learning programs could be started in schools in your community, you can find out how. If you're a health-care practitioner or interested in improving your own health or working with a chronic condition through mindfulness, you will find helpful information. Likewise, if you are a military service member, or in any uniformed service, you can find people who can help you increase your mental fitness. If you would like to learn more about groups applying mindful approaches to our challenges in the inner city, or with birth or parenting, or with the environment, or the workplace, or climate change, the resource section can get you started.

Thanks for listening. I hope we can meet someday. And as my grandfather used to say, "Just do the best you can."

AFTERWORD

Mindfulness and Kindness Practices
by Dr. Susan Bauer-Wu

Living amid the busyness of our high-tech and low-touch society can sometimes take us away from fully experiencing our day-to-day lives. We often live on autopilot, *doing* without *experiencing*. We can be quick to judge, react, resist, run away, or retreat when things don't go smoothly or the way we want.

Mindfulness is opening up to now, whatever is happening—within you and around you, pleasant or unpleasant. It can be cultivated through practices that help stabilize the mind. Intentionally paying attention to a neutral point of focus is the easiest way to stabilize the mind, like an anchor that stops a boat from drifting aimlessly or getting tossed around in a storm. At a moment's notice, you can return to the experience of the present moment simply by bringing awareness to an easily accessible point of focus.

In mindfulness practice, the breath is often used as an anchor, the neutral point of awareness that drops us into now. The breath is always with us. It is just there, a trusty companion, with us every moment we are alive. We don't have to try to breathe; it just happens, much as the waves of the ocean continue to meet the shore. So any place and any time you feel agitated, confused, sluggish, apathetic, or overwhelmed, the breath can be your anchor.

MINDFULNESS PRACTICE: AWARENESS OF BREATHING

Do this practice at a time of day and location when you're unlikely to have interruptions or feel sleepy. It may mean that you close your office door and turn off your phone and computer in the middle of the work day, or you get up 15 minutes earlier in the morning, or in the evening you go into a separate room in your home and ask your family to not disturb you for a little while.

There is no need to have a particular goal in mind. You're not trying to feel a certain way, do anything special, or get anything specific out of it. You're simply being present with yourself by stilling the body, tuning in, and quieting the mind for a few minutes. The instructions below present a breathing practice you can do over and over again whenever you choose. You can find more details about the practice in the books mentioned at the beginning of the resource section.

- Settle into a steady and comfortable sitting posture—in a chair or on a cushion on the floor. The back is relatively straight, but not rigid, allowing breathing to be open and easy. Hands can be placed on the thighs or resting loosely together on the lap. The head and neck are balanced. You may either close your eyes or just lower them with a soft gaze.

- Bring your awareness to the sensation of your body touching the chair or cushion, your feet touching the floor, the feeling of the air in the room.

- Gently bring awareness to the breath as it moves in and out.

- Notice where the breath is most vivid for you. This may be at the nostrils or at the chest as it rises and falls, or maybe right at the belly. You may choose to place your hand on your belly as you notice the expanding and releasing.

- You may be aware of the brief pause between the in-breath and the out-breath.

- Notice the rhythm of your breathing, and be aware of the sensations of the air coming into and filling your body, and then releasing itself and leaving your body.

- Stay present with the experience of breathing. Just allow yourself to breathe in a natural and comfortable way, riding the waves of in-breath and out-breath.

- If your attention has wandered off the breath (and it will), gently escort it back to awareness of breathing. Allow thoughts or emotions to arise without pushing them away or holding on to them. Simply observe them with a very light and gentle curiosity. No need to get carried away by them, or to judge or interpret them.

- That's it.

MINDFULNESS PRACTICE: BODY AWARENESS (OR BODY SCAN)

Here is a wonderful practice that helps ground you and tune you in to your body, experiencing it just as it is right now. You may do this practice sitting in a chair or on the floor, lying down, or standing.

- Allow yourself to settle into a comfortable position in which you feel supported and relaxed, yet will not lead you to fall asleep.

- You may close your eyes or keep them slightly open with a soft gaze, not focusing on anything in particular.

- Rest for a few moments in awareness of the natural rhythm of your breathing.

- Once your body and mind are settled, bring awareness to your body as a whole. Be aware of your body resting and being supported by the chair, mattress, or floor.

- Bring awareness to different parts of your body. You may choose to focus on one particular area of the body or scan your body in a sequence like this one: toes, feet (sole, heel, top of foot), through the legs, pelvis, abdomen, lower back, upper back, chest, shoulders, arms down to the fingers, shoulders, neck, different parts of the face and head.

- For each part of the body, linger for a few moments and notice the different sensations, their quality, intensity, and constancy.

- The moment you notice that your mind has wandered, return your attention to the part of the body you last remember.

If you fall asleep when you do the body scan, that's okay. Your mind and body have let go enough to drift off and give you needed rest and recuperation. When you notice that you fell asleep, take a deep breath to reawaken your body, reposition your body if necessary (which may help wake it up), and, when you are ready, return your attention to the part of the body you last remember.

KINDNESS PRACTICE

You can learn to open your heart and cultivate kindness and goodwill toward others and yourself through practices that send out sincere good wishes to all. When you take a little time to do these practices and cultivate unconditional goodwill, you will likely feel a greater sense of well-being and be more connected with others and the world around you.

Bring to mind someone toward whom you'd like to extend feelings of kindness, love, and goodness. This may be someone dear to you, an acquaintance, someone with whom you have difficulty, a stranger, or yourself. Many people find it easier to begin with someone they love, and later practice kindness toward people they feel neutral toward or even dislike. Silently repeat the following phrases (or use words that feel right to you) in such a way that the words resonate, so you can feel them in your heart.

May you be free from harm.

May you be free from worry, fear, and anger.

May you be happy.

May you be physically healthy and strong.

May you live with ease.

A Simple Tip to Spark Mindfulness

An easy way to remember how to be mindful in the course of a busy day, or when you are overwhelmed, preoccupied, worried, angry, or uncomfortable, is to STOP:

S—Stop. Simply pause from what you are doing.

T—Take a few slow, deep breaths with awareness and tune in.

O—Observe and curiously notice your thoughts, feelings, and sensations.

P—Proceed with whatever you were doing, with awareness and kindness.

Bringing Mindfulness into Everyday Life

The activities of daily living all provide great opportunities to discover mindfulness. You can brush your teeth, take a shower, or shave with a keen quality of attention and care. You can eat mindfully—noticing smells, tastes, textures, and temperatures, and what it feels like to chew and swallow. You can pay more attention when you're driving, noticing your reactions to other drivers and traffic. You can bring awareness to household chores, to walking upstairs and downstairs, to taking out the garbage.

When someone is talking to you, listen fully and do nothing else. Connect with nature by going outside or looking out the window. Notice the color of the sky, the movement and shape of clouds, the stars, the moon, cool air or mist on your face, the sounds of animals. You will soon find that paying attention is not a chore. It's refreshing and invigorating.

RESOURCES FOR MINDFULNESS TRAINING, APPLIED MINDFULNESS, AND MINDFUL SOCIAL ACTION

The organizations, books, websites, online courses and videos, audio files and CDs, and other media recommended in this section can help you learn more about the practice of mindfulness and how to apply it in various aspects of life.

GENERAL RESOURCES

Books

The Craving Mind: From Cigarettes to Smartphones to Love: Why We Get Hooked and How We Can Break Bad Habits
Judson Brewer • Yale University 2017

The Emotional Life of Your Brain: How Its Unique Patterns Affect the Way You Think, Feel, and Live—and How You Can Change Them
Richard J. Davidson and Sharon Begley • Hudson Street 2012

Full Catastrophe Living: Using the Wisdom of Your Body and Mind to Face Stress, Pain, and Illness, 15th anniversary edition
Jon Kabat-Zinn • Delta 2009

Fully Present: The Science, Art, and Practice of Mindfulness
Susan Smalley and Diana Winston • Da Capo 2010

Leaves Falling Gently: Living Fully with Serious and Life-Limiting Illness through Mindfulness, Compassion, and Connectedness
Susan Bauer-Wu • New Harbinger 2011

The Mindful Brain: Reflection and Attunement in the Cultivation of Well-Being
Daniel J. Siegel • W. W. Norton 2007

The Mindful Manifesto: How Doing Less and Noticing More Can Help Us Thrive in a Stressed-Out World
Jonty Heaversedge and Ed Halliwell • Hay House 2012

The Mindfulness Revolution: Leading Psychologists, Scientists, Artists, and Meditation Teachers on the Power of Mindfulness in Daily Life
Barry Boyce (editor) • Shambhala 2011

A Mindfulness-Based Stress Reduction Workbook
Elisha Goldstein and Bob Stahl • New Harbinger 2010

The Now Effect: How a Mindful Moment Can Change the Rest of Your Life
Elisha Goldstein • Atria 2013

Real Happiness: The Power of Meditation: A 28-Day Program
Sharon Salzberg • Workman 2010

Search Inside Yourself: The Unexpected Path to Achieving Success, Happiness (and World Peace)
Chade-Meng Tan • HarperCollins 2014

Ten Mindful Minutes: Giving Our Children—and Ourselves—the Social and Emotional Skills to Reduce Stress and Anxiety for Healthier, Happy Lives
Goldie Hawn • Penguin 2011

10% Happier: How I Tamed the Voice in My Head, Reduced Stress Without Losing My Edge, and Found Self-Help That Actually Works—A True Story
Dan Harris • HarperCollins 2014

Train Your Mind, Change Your Brain: How a New Science Reveals Our Extraordinary Potential to Transform Ourselves
Sharon Begley • Ballantine 2007

Wherever You Go, There You Are: Mindfulness Meditation in Everyday Life, 10th anniversary edition
Jon Kabat-Zinn • Hyperion 2005

Mindfulness Apps

Mindful Magazine

An accompaniment to the print magazine, the *Mindful* magazine app offers articles from leading thinkers, researchers, and teachers in the mindfulness world. The app is available on iOS and Android. With the free download, users can read a limited number of articles per month. A subscription option is available in the app.

Headspace

Headspace features guided meditations in time frames as short as two minutes and as long as an hour. It also offers meditations for specific issues, such as anxiety and relationships. The app is available for desktop, iPad, iPhone, and Android. There is a free 10-day trial, after which users can subscribe for a monthly fee.

10% Happier

Created by Dan Harris, the 10% Happier app has guided meditations led by reputable mindfulness teachers. The meditations cover topics such as how to cope with anxiety, political stress, or sleeplessness. The app works on the iPad, iPhone, and Android. There is a free version, as well as the option to subscribe for a monthly fee.

Inner Explorer

An adjunct to the Inner Explorer mindfulness program for school-children, the Inner Explorer app allows parents to connect with the techniques their children are learning in the classroom and share in the experience with a home version of the Inner Explorer classroom program. The app is available on iOS and Android mobile devices for a monthly or yearly subscription fee after a 30-day free trial period.

Calm

The Calm app is specifically geared toward relaxation. Calm offers several services, including a timer for silent meditation, guided meditations, and relaxing nature sounds. A handful of programs are free, and there are subscription options to unlock the others. Available for iOS and Android mobile devices.

Whil

Whil is geared toward mindfulness in teams or in the workplace, drawn from neuroscience and behavioral science. Available for desktop, Android, iPhone, or iPad. Mindfulness sessions provide meditation and awareness. Whil also includes video yoga sessions. The app is free, with a paid subscription option.

Audio and Video

These media provide guided instruction in mindfulness practice or discussion of the benefits of mindfulness, either online or available on CD.

Tara Brach

Audio CD: *Mindfulness Meditation: Nine Guided Practices to Awaken Presence and Open Your Heart.* Sounds True 2012.

Center for Mindfulness in Medicine, Health Care, and Society

www.umassmed.edu/cfm/products.aspx

Philippe Goldin

"The Cognitive Neuroscience of Mindfulness Meditation," a talk by Philippe Goldin, Ph.D. (Googletech Talks) www.youtube.com/watch?v=sf6Q0G1iHBI

Elisha Goldstein

"STOP: A Short Mindfulness Practice" from *A Mindfulness-Based Stress Reduction Workbook.* Video presentation at the MBSR Workbook channel. www.youtube.com/watch?v=PhwQvEGmF_I

MP3 download: *Mindfulness Solutions for Stress, Anxiety, and Depression* http://elishagoldstein.com/audio/mindful-solutions-for-stress-anxiety-and-depression

Jon Kabat-Zinn

Audio CD: *Guided Mindfulness Meditation.* Sounds True, 2005. Audio CD: *Mindfulness for Beginners.* Sounds True, 2006. "Mindfulness with Jon Kabat-Zinn." Video of talk and guided meditation at Google. www.youtube.com/watch?v=3nwwKbM_vJc

UCLA Mindful Awareness Research Center Mindful Meditation:

downloadable podcasts www.marc.ucla.edu/body.cfm?id=22

UC San Diego Health System

Guided Audio Files to Practice Mindfulness-Based Stress Reduction health.ucsd.edu/specialties/mindfulness/programs/mbsr/Pages/audio.aspx

Pam Weiss

Appropriate Response Guided Meditation: five-minute MP3 audio https://www.appropriateresponse.com/teachings/#anchor-guided_meditations

Distance Education: Online Courses in Mindfulness

These organizations teach mindfulness practice (and the science behind it) through virtual classroom software, web conferencing, and other live or prerecorded formats. Check the websites for course schedules and fees; some programs offer financial aid. Web page content may be subject to change. For more information, use the phone numbers and e-mail addresses provided below.

Duke Integrative Medicine

The Mindful Way to Reduce Stress: A Distance Learning Program. Weekly classes via telephone conference.
https://www.dukeintegrativemedicine.org/programs-training/public/mindfulness-based-stressed-reduction-distance-learning
(866) 313-0959 (toll-free) or (919) 660-6826 (local call, Durham, NC)
info@dukeintegrativemedicine.org

eMindful

Large variety of courses via virtual online classroom using live streaming video, audio, and chat. Programs available for specific concerns, including stress reduction, cancer, shyness, chronic pain, mindful eating, conflict resolution, and more.
www.emindful.com
(855) 211-1529
info@eMindful.com

Mindful Living Programs

MBSR intensive real-time course via virtual classroom software
http://www.mindfullivingprograms.com/mbsr_online_schedule.php
(530) 898-1495 (Chico, CA)
steve@mindfullivingprograms.com (Steve Flowers)

Mindfulness Awareness Research Center (MARC)

UCLA Semel Institute for Neuroscience and Human Behavior
Prerecorded online course with audio and video materials, plus live chat
www.marc.ucla.edu
(310) 206-7503 (Los Angeles, CA)
marcinfo@ucla.edu

Mindsight Institute

Neuroscience-based courses with Dr. Dan Siegel about how the mind, brain, and interpersonal relationships work together to contribute to our well-being

Prerecorded lectures plus live discussions with Dr. Siegel
www.mind sightinstitute.com/online_courses
(310) 447-0848 (Los Angeles, CA)
onlinecourses@mindsightinstitute.com

The Penn Program for Mindfulness
Contact the program for news of online classes coming soon.
http://www.pennmedicine.org/stress
(800)-789-PENN (789-7366) (toll-free)
mindfulness@uphs.upenn.edu
To join mailing list: stress.management@uphs.upenn.edu

Research

The following websites and publications offer articles,
reports, audio, and video on mindfulness research and
mindfulness practice.

American Mindfulness Research Association

Electronic resource and publication database providing information
to researchers, practitioners, and the general public on the scientific
study of mindfulness, including the *Mindfulness Research Monthly*
goamra.org

Center for Healthy Minds

Waisman Center, University of Wisconsin–Madison
Regular updates on neuroscience research on mindfulness and contemplative practices. Read articles, participate in studies, sign up for
newsletter.
www.investigatinghealthyminds.org/cihmfindings.html

Greater Good: The Science of a Meaningful Life

The Greater Good Science Center, UC Berkeley
Quarterly online magazine reporting on the psychology, sociology,
and neuroscience of well-being. Free videos and podcasts.
www.greatergood.berkeley.edu

Mindful: Healthy Mind, Healthy Life

Print magazine published six times per year plus a website that
includes mindfulness instruction, audio and video, and reports on
innovative mindfulness programs and research results
www.mindful.org

RESOURCES FOR CHAPTERS 3–8

Science (Chapter 3: What Scientists Say Mindfulness Can Do for You)

CCARE: The Center for Compassion and Altruism Research and Education (James Doty)
ccare.stanford.edu

CIHM: Center for Healthy Minds (Richard Davidson)
www.investigatinghealthyminds.org

The Greater Good Science Center (Dacher Keltner, Ph.D.)
greatergood.berkeley.edu/about
Book: *Born to Be Good: The Science of a Meaningful Life*
Dacher Keltner • W. W. Norton 2009

Rick Hanson, Ph.D.
Wellspring Institute for Neuroscience and Contemplative Wisdom
www.rickhanson.net/home/wellspring

Amishi P. Jha, Ph.D.
The Jha Lab
www.amishi.com/lab

Jon Kabat-Zinn, Ph.D.
Center for Mindfulness in Medicine, Health Care, and Society
University of Massachusetts Medical School
https://www.umassmed.edu/cfm/about-us/people/2-meet-our
-faculty/kabat-zinn-profile/

Education (Chapter 4: How Mindfulness Can Increase Our Children's Attention and Kindness)

Association for Mindfulness in Education
www.mindfuleducation.org

CASEL: Collaborative for Academic, Social, and Emotional Learning (Linda Lantieri, M.A.)
www.casel.org

The Center for Contemplative Mind in Society
www.contemplativemind.org

Contemplative Studies Initiative & Concentration (Hal Roth, Ph.D.)
www.brown.edu/Faculty/Contemplative_Studies_Initiative

Cultivating Awareness and Resilience in Education
www.garrisoninstitute.org/index.php?option=com_content
&view=article&id=77&Itemid=79

Goldie Hawn
The Hawn Foundation: MindUP program
www.thehawnfoundation.org/mindup

Inner Explorer
https://innerexplorer.org

The Inner Kids Program (Susan Kaiser Greenland)
https://www.susankaisergreenland.com/inner-kids-program
Book: *The Mindful Child: How to Help Your Kid Manage Stress and Become Happier, Kinder, and More Compassionate*
Susan Kaiser Greenland • Atria 2010
Book: *Mindful Games: Sharing Mindfulness and Meditation with Children, Teens, and Families*
Susan Kaiser Greenland • Shambhala 2017

Mindful Schools
www.mindfulschools.org

Mindfulness and Emotional Intelligence (Daniel Goleman, Ph.D.)
www.danielgoleman.info
Book: *Building Emotional Intelligence: Practices to Cultivate Inner Resilience in Children*
Linda Lantieri, with practices guided by Daniel Goleman • Sounds True 2014

Social and Emotional Learning
George Lucas Foundation
www.edutopia.org
Under the tab "Videos," select the topic "Social and Emotional Learning."

Other Books on Education and Parenting

Everyday Blessings: The Inner Work of Mindful Parenting, revised and updated
Myla and John Kabat-Zinn • Hachette 2014

Mindful Teacher, Mindful School: Improving Wellbeing in
Teaching and Learning
Kevin Hawkins • SAGE 2017

Mindful Teaching and Teaching Mindfulness: A Guide for Anyone
Who Teaches Anything
Deborah Schoeberlein David and Suki Sheth • Wisdom 2009

Mindfulness for Teachers: Simple Skills for Peace and Productivity
in the Classroom
Patricia Jennings • W.W. Norton 2015

No-Drama Discipline: The Whole-Brain Way to Calm the Chaos
and Nurture Your Child's Developing Mind
Daniel J. Siegel • Bantam 2016

Health Care (Chapter 5: How Mindfulness Can Improve Our Health and Our Health-Care System)

Center for Mindfulness in Medicine, Health Care, and Society
(Saki Santorelli, Ed.D.)
www.umassmed.edu/cfm/index.aspx
Book: *Heal Thy Self: Lessons on Mindfulness in Medicine*
Saki Santorelli • Harmony 2000

Christiane Northrup, M.D.
www.drnorthrup.com
Book: *Women's Bodies, Women's Wisdom: Creating Physical and
Emotional Health and Healing*
Christiane Northrup • Bantam 2010

Duke University Integrative Medicine (Jeff Brantley)
www.dukeintegrativemedicine.org
Book: *Calming Your Anxious Mind: How Mindfulness and Compassion
Can Free You from Anxiety, Fear, and Panic*
Jeffrey Brantley • New Harbinger 2007

Optimal Weight for Life (OWL) Program at Children's Hospital
(David Ludwig, M.D.)
http://www.childrenshospital.org/centers-and-services/optimal
-weight-for-life-program

Stress Reduction Program
Center for Mindfulness in Medicine, Health Care, and Society
www.umassmed.edu/cfm/mindfulness-based-programs

Other Books on Mindfulness and Health

Attending: Medicine, Mindfulness, and Humanity
Ronald Epstein, M.D. • Scribner 2017

Mindful Eating: A Guide to Rediscovering a Healthy and Joyful Relationship with Food (includes CD), revised
Jan Chozen Bays • Shambhala 2017

Mindfulness-Based Therapy for Insomnia
Jason Ong • American Psychological Association 2016

How to Live Well with Chronic Pain and Illness: A Mindful Guide
Toni Bernhard • Wisdom 2015

The Joy of Half a Cookie: Using Mindfulness to Lose Weight and End the Struggle with Food
Jean Kristeller • Perigee 2015

You Are Not Your Pain: Using Mindfulness to Relieve Pain, Reduce Stress and Restore Well-Being
Vidyamala Burch and Danny Penman • Flatiron 2015

Military, Veterans, and First Responders (Chapter 6: How Mindfulness Can Improve Performance and Build Resiliency for Our Military and First Responders)

Center for Contemplative Mind in Society (Mirabai Bush)
www.contemplativemind.org

Military Care Providers Project
The Use of Meditation and Mindfulness Practices to Support Military Care Providers: A Prospectus
A publication of the Center for Contemplative Mind in Society
www.contemplativemind.org/admin/wp-content/uploads/2012/09/MeditationforCareProviders.pdf

Posttraumatic Stress Disorder (PTSD)
National Center for PTSD (Tony King, Ph.D.)
U.S. Department of Veterans Affairs
www.ptsd.va.gov

Veteran Health and Well-Being Programs and Research
Center for Healthy Minds
centerhealthyminds.org/science/studies/veteran-wellness-study

Leadership and the Environment (Chapter 7: How Mindfulness Can Help Us Rediscover Our Values and Reshape Our Economy)

Appropriate Response (Pam Weiss)
www.appropriateresponse.com

Baltimore Neighborhood Energy Challenge (Alice Kennedy)
baltimoreenergychallenge.org

The Center for Green Schools
www.centerforgreenschools.org/home

Claremont Graduate University
Peter F. Drucker and Masatoshi Ito Graduate School of Management
Jeremy Hunter teaches courses and does research on the practice of
self-management, using mindfulness to increase resiliency, focus,
judgment, decision-making, communication, and quality of life.
www.cgu.edu/jeremy-hunter

The Climate and Energy Project
www.climateandenergy.org

Climate, Mind and Behavior Program (Jonathan Rose)
Garrison Institute
www.garrisoninstitute.org/index.php?option=com_content&view
=article&id=244&Itemid=1071

Daniel J. Siegel, M.D.
Mindsight Institute
www.mindsightinstitute.com
See also entry for Mindsight Institute under "Distance Education"
above.

Global Green
www.globalgreen.org

Green for All (Van Jones)
www.greenforall.org
Book: *The Green Collar Economy: How One Solution Can Fix Our
Two Biggest Problems*
Van Jones • HarperOne 2009

Institute for Mindful Leadership (Janice Marturano)

www.instituteformindfulleadership.org

Paul Hawken, Environmental Activist

www.paulhawken.com
Book: *Blessed Unrest: How the Largest Social Movement in History Is
Restoring Grace, Justice, and Beauty to the World*
Paul Hawken • Penguin 2008

Society for Organizational Learning (Peter Senge, M.S., Ph.D.)

www.solonline.org/organizational-learning-2
Book: *The Necessary Revolution: How Individuals and Organizations
Are Working Together to Create a Sustainable World*
Peter Senge • Crown Business 2010

Social Services (Chapter 8: How Mindfulness Can Help Us Help Ourselves and Our Country)

The Berkana Institute

Community-based problem solving, under the direction of Meg
Wheatley
www.berkana.org

Charter for Compassion (Karen Armstrong)

www.charterforcompassion.org
Book: *Twelve Steps to a Compassionate Life*
Karen Armstrong • Knopf 2010

**Holistic Life Foundation, Inc. (Atman & Ali Smith and Andres
Gonzales)**

www.hlfinc.org

Mind Body Awareness Project

www.mbaproject.org

Mindfulness Without Borders

Inspires students, parents, educators, and professionals to make positive social change across cultures.
mindfulnesswithoutborders.org

**Mindfulness-Based Childbirth and Parenting (MBCP) Program
(Nancy Bardacke, C.N.M., M.A.)**

www.mindfulbirthing.org
Book: *Mindful Birthing: Training the Mind, Body, and Heart for
Childbirth and Beyond*
Nancy Bardacke • HarperOne 2012

Mindfulness-Based Relapse Prevention
http://www.mindfulrp.com
Book: *Mindfulness-Based Relapse Prevention for Addictive Behaviors: A Clinician's Guide*
Sarah Bowen, Neha Chawla, and G. Alan Marlatt • Guilford 2010

Stressed Teens (Gina M. Biegel, M.A., L.M.F.T.)
www.stressedteens.com
Book (ages 12 up): *The Stress Reduction Workbook for Teens: Mindfulness Skills to Help You Deal with Stress*
Gina Biegel • Instant Help/New Harbinger 2017

Thomas Homer-Dixon
Researcher concerned with threats to global security and on how societies adapt to complex economic, ecological, and technological change.
www.homerdixon.com
Book: *The Upside of Down: Catastrophe, Creativity, and the Renewal of Civilization*
Thomas Homer-Dixon • Island Press 2008

Other Books on Mental Health and Addiction

The Mindful Path through Shyness: How Mindfulness and Compassion Can Help Free You from Social Anxiety, Fear, and Avoidance
Steve Flowers • New Harbinger 2009

Mindful Recovery: A Spiritual Path to Healing from Addiction
Thomas Bien and Beverly Bien • Wiley 2002

The Mindful Way Through Anxiety: Break Free from Chronic Worry and Reclaim Your Life
Susan M. Orsillo and Lizabeth Roemer • Guilford 2011

Mindfulness-Based Cognitive Therapy for Depression: A New Approach to Preventing Relapse, 2nd edition
Zindel Segal, Mark Williams, and John Teasdale • Guilford 2013

The Mindfulness-Based Emotional Balance Workbook
Margaret Cullen and Ganzalo Brito Pons • New Harbinger 2015

Present Perfect: A Mindfulness Approach to Letting Go of Perfectionism and the Need for Control
Pavel Somov • New Harbinger 2010

APPENDIX A
Religious and Spiritual Mindful Practices

CENTERING PRAYER

This meditative practice has been especially popular with Christians who would like to incorporate a mindfulness element into their spiritual life.

The website Contemplative Outreach defines centering prayer as ". . . a receptive method of silent prayer that prepares us to receive the gift of contemplative prayer, prayer in which we experience God's presence within us, closer than breathing, closer than thinking, closer than consciousness itself. This method of prayer is both a relationship with God and a discipline to foster that relationship.

"Centering Prayer is not meant to replace other kinds of prayer. Rather, it adds depth of meaning to all prayer and facilitates the movement from more active modes of prayer—verbal, mental or affective prayer— into a receptive prayer of resting in God. Centering Prayer emphasizes prayer as a personal relationship with God and as a movement beyond conversation with Christ to communion with Christ." See www .contemplativeoutreach.org.

In his book *The Purpose Driven Life*, Pastor Rick Warren encourages a form of meditation he describes as *"focused* thinking. It takes serious effort. You select a verse and reflect on it over and over in your mind . . . if you know how to worry, you already know how to meditate."

Transcendental Meditation and Other Practices from Hindu Tradition

In the Western world, the most widely known practice that developed from Hindu traditions is Transcendental Meditation (TM). Maharishi Mahesh Yogi developed this technique, drawing India's ancient (pre-Hindu) Vedic traditions into the 20th century. He brought the technique to the United States in the 1960s. TM includes the use of a mantra—a word or sound used to focus the concentration—and is intended to be practiced for around 20 minutes per day. Notably, some practitioners approach this practice from a religious perspective and others from a secular way of thinking.

There are many variations of contemplative practices that have developed within and outside of Hindu tradition. Vedic meditation, for example, is very similar and is, in fact, the more ancient practice from which Transcendental Meditation is mostly derived.

The David Lynch Foundation promotes TM for health and well-being and has a wide variety of programs for schoolchildren and other groups, such as veterans and prisoners, under the banner of "Healing Traumatic Stress and Raising Performance in At-Risk Populations."

For more information, see www.webmd.com, www.themeditationtrust.com, www.tm.org, and www.davidlynchfoundation.org.

Jewish Contemplative Practice

Judaism includes several distinct contemplative traditions, including Kaballah, Jewish Science, and Jews who practice within Unitarian Universalist congregations, among others. The Society of Jewish Science Center for

Applied Judaism summarizes the value of meditation throughout Jewish sects as follows:

"In Judaism, in the Sacred Scriptures, it is said that prayer (or meditation) enables us to open a clear channel between the Divine Mind and the human mind, it allows us to connect and become as one. We tap the inner resources of our soul wherein God resides; in this silence and kinship, in this state of divine closeness, rests the opportunity to affirm for help, and to receive help. Whatever we need or desire, either for ourselves, or for someone else, God hears our call, our prayer; and our prayers, when offered earnestly and wholeheartedly, are always answered. It is in the silence of our minds that God can hear us best. [. . .] A meditation can be in the form of a worded or imaged prayer taken from the Scriptures, or a worded or imaged thought or prayer of your own choosing."

For more information on Jewish Science, see thecenterforappliedjudaism.org/prayer/meditation.

For information on Kaballah, see www.kabbalah.info /engkab/openeng.htm#.WlKC5d-nHIU.

For information on Jewish Unitarian Universalists, see www.uua.org/beliefs/what-we-believe/beliefs/judaism.

MEDITATION IN YOGA (SAVASANA)

Savasana is a Sanskrit word meaning "corpse pose." It is the final posture taken at the end of any yoga session. Savasana is practiced by lying down (on the floor or yoga mat), face up to the sky, with your eyes closed and body consciously relaxed.

"*Savasana* . . . is a peak pose," according to Yoga International. "It isn't just filler time or time to grab a quick nap before hustling back to our busy lives. The purpose of savasana is to learn to just be, a colossal challenge. Savasana can be practiced in many ways, including focusing awareness on the breath or guided muscle relaxation. The mind has a tendency to wander or check out and go to sleep, but the practice of savasana trains our minds to observe and be aware of the stillness inherent in each and every moment. In savasana, we relax into the room, the mat, and ourselves and then try to let go of everything surrounding us. We release internal thoughts and move into a place of non-judgmental acceptance and awareness. This time of mindfulness is beneficial to every part of our being."

For more information, see www.yogainternational.com.

BUDDHIST MEDITATION

Mindfulness meditation is a core component of most traditions of Buddhism. According to the website Lion's Roar: "The Buddha taught meditation as an essential tool to achieve liberation from suffering. Additionally, we might meditate to specifically cultivate certain positive traits, like friendliness, steadiness, compassion, and joy. . . . Buddhist practice always starts with meditations that calm and concentrate the mind; what often follows is insight, Buddhism's unique specialty. With the stable, focused, and fully present mind you have developed in your mindfulness practice, you can begin to investigate the nature of reality." See www.lionsroar.com.

ISLAMIC CONTEMPLATIVE PRACTICES

There are a variety of contemplative practices in Islam. These include reflecting upon lines of scripture, visualizing the Creator, "checking in" with the breath and sensations in the body, and conscious breathing.

The Islamic Insights website says: "Meditation in Islam can be described as the development of the presence of body, heart, and mind in worship and religious contemplation. It is essential to spiritual development and acceptance of and benefit from prayers. [. . .]"

As Omid Safi, Director of Duke University's Islamic Studies Center, tells *Mindful* magazine: "To pray with the heart, to have presence in the heart, is a remedy. It is a healing, an un-scattering. Presence is simply to have our heart be where our feet are. This starts with a mindfulness, with an awareness of the breath. When we monitor our breath, simply observe the breath enter into the heart, and emerge from the heart, our breathing slows down. The heart rate slows down. Here is where we become whole: our body, our breath, our spirit become One."

See onbeing.org/blog/the-prayer-of-the-heart and www.islamicinsights.com.

Native American Mindfulness

Elements of mindfulness are encompassed within some Native American spiritual traditions, both historically and in the present. The Tapestry Institute's website outlines these elements: "Mindful awareness has three major components: (1) being fully present in the moment, rather than focusing on either the past or the future; (2) being aware of the thoughts, emotions, and experiences that arise in that present moment; and (3) being nonjudgmental when those thoughts, emotions, and experiences arise. These components of mindfulness are important to a number of traditional Indigenous cultures, although formal transmission of the skill is not as well-developed as it is in some of the other cultures where it's found."

In a *Mindful* magazine interview with Renda Dionne, a member of the Turtle Mountain Band of Chippewa Indians and a mindfulness teacher certified by the UCLA Mindful Awareness Research Center who does mindfulness work with Native American families, she tells us: "'All My Relations' . . . is central to the Native American worldview, and it's related to being in balance and understanding our inherent interconnectedness. That deep interconnectedness is one of the most profound ways that mindfulness fits within the American Indian way of looking at things. In traditional times, Native Americans lived naturally in the present moment. But today our attention is spread over so many things, and there is so much stimulation coming at us all the time, that those parts of our brain don't get as developed, and we have difficulty finding our balance.

". . . For American Indians stories are medicine. In relation to mindfulness, storytelling involves being present with yourself and the audience, and speaking from the heart. We practice both mindful speaking and mindful listening within a story circle, as well as improvisational games. In a mindfulness setting, storytelling helps people connect with their intuition. Speaking truth helps separate our conditioning from our intuitive wisdom. I emphasize the traditional Native American wisdom and traditional ways of knowing, and how that relates to present moment awareness—mindfulness."

See tapestryinstitute.org.

APPENDIX B

Seven Reminders for Mindful Eating

LET THE FORK LINGER

Try not to let your fork or spoon become a shovel. Take a pause as you pick up your food, a half moment to appreciate it before putting it in your mouth.

USE ALL YOUR SENSES

Eating is not just about taste buds. Fruits and vegetables are natural works of art. There are color, shape, texture, coolness, heat, crunch, and many other facets to appreciate that make a meal a total sensory experience. If you like, you can take a moment to be thankful for everyone who made it possible for you to be eating this food.

GO FOR THE YUM FACTOR

Let the taste of the food put the brakes on your speedy, wandering mind. When food tastes good and you're really paying attention, it can stop you for a second. And if you're eating something that's more ordinary than yummy, appreciate the simplicity.

COME BACK

Just as in any mindfulness practice, you will find that your mind has wandered off. No big deal. Just as you would use the breath in a formal meditation practice, use the taste and the look of the food as the anchor in the present to come back to. Repeat as needed.

Listen to Your Stomach

It takes a moment for your body to let you know that you've become full and satisfied. If you slow down even more as the meal progresses, there's a better chance you'll hear it when the bell goes off to signal that you are done. If there's something left over, you can wrap it up and save it for another time.

Enjoy the Pause

Our days are often filled with rushing from one thing to the next or constantly relating to something on a screen. A meal can provide a complete break from that. Find a nice spot, settle in, and take your time with it. If you're with others, savor the conversation, but don't let it carry you completely away from the sensory delights of your meal.

Commit!

Try, when you can, to decide about how much to take and which foods to eat before you start to eat. If you're second-guessing yourself while you're eating, it just stirs up anxiety, which is not great for digestion and habit building. Take half a slice of pumpkin pie and commit to totally enjoying it.

From mindful.org

ENDNOTES

Chapter 1

1. In the years since that address, we have seen lots of innovation, but that innovation is not getting to large swaths of the country. The small and midsize cities, towns, and rural areas bear the costs of using the innovations created in larger centers, but they see little local investment in innovative industry while jobs in their traditional industries keep disappearing. Yes, our workers need to adapt, but even more importantly, our leaders need to adapt to the reality of the investment divide and find ways to bring innovation and investment to all parts of our country: urban, suburban, exurban, rural. The money cannot all flow in the direction of the tech centers and leave the rest of the country behind.

Chapter 2

2. When I first wrote this book, it was before a fearmonger was elected President. Candidate Trump did manage to scare people by pointing to genuine economic insecurities that people were experiencing and still are, and many people thought, "Let's give it a try; maybe he can fix it." But he has continued to use this tactic of scaring and polarizing—pointing to other people who are the problem, who are less "American" than you or me—and it's wearing thin for people now, including many who voted for him. If you choose to use fear and divisiveness, they can get you elected, but as a long-term strategy for governing, it never works out. Fear is exhausting and debilitating.

Chapter 5

3. An important aspect of health care and self-care is our ability to pay attention to how we eat, what we eat, and where it comes from, which is why I wrote the book *The Real Food Revolution* in 2015. There are lots of good resources on mindful eating practices, a few of which are mentioned in the resources section at the end

of the book. Appendix B contains some simple guidelines for mindful eating from www.mindful.org.

Chapter 8

4. A few years after the release of the first edition of this book, Vinny Ferraro and Chris McKenna turned over the leadership of the MBA program to their colleague Mary Stancavage and went on to do great work with Mindful Schools (mentioned in Chapter 4). Vinny remains a member of the MBA board and Chris is on the advisory council.

ACKNOWLEDGMENTS

As I look back on my life, I'm moved by the generosity of many people who went out of their way to help me through difficult times and provide mentorship and inspiration. They instilled an optimism that continues to inspire me about the future of our country and the world. Since many are gone or beyond my reach, this book is my attempt to pay it forward.

I would like to thank Jon Kabat-Zinn for teaching me the power of mindfulness, helping me understand a little better what it means to be human, and being the spark that began the mindfulness movement in America. He inspires in others the courage to walk confidently into "the full catastrophe." I'm deeply grateful for his mentorship, love, and inspiration during the writing of this book and for introducing me to many of the people described here.

As I've said in the book, the people I've met who are applying mindfulness in so many different aspects of our society are genuine heroes. They are taking it to the streets, and we all owe them a debt of gratitude. It's their grassroots work that will attract other citizens and be the catalyst for a more mindful nation. I'm appreciative that they gave so generously of their time and wisdom. If even a few readers are inspired to do what these heroes are doing, this book will be a big success.

Huge thanks to my developmental editor, Barry Boyce, and my project agent, James Gimian—two of the people who created mindful.org. They believed in what I wanted to do when this project was only a few notes sketched on napkins. Barry's editorial precision, grace, tenacity, and fine sense for what mindfulness really means made this book a reality. Jimmy always seems to see life's big picture and identify unseen opportunities. Thanks to his many readings of the manuscript, this is a much better book. He tied the room together.

Enormous thanks are due to my literary agent, Stephanie Tade, for lifting up the vision of this book and always challenging me to think bigger and bolder. Many thanks to Reid Tracy, President and CEO of Hay House, for believing in this project so wholeheartedly as soon as he read the proposal, and for advocating it so strongly. My editor at Hay House, Patty Gift, showed a deft hand and razor-sharp insight. Her passion for this project kept me motivated as we dealt with the many challenges of finishing a book. Thanks also to all the people at Hay House who leaned their shoulders into this effort. I'm lucky to have such an energetic, talented team behind this book.

I want to thank the team of research and editorial assistants we assembled to pull together all the information and help turn drafts into a manuscript and finally into a book. Thanks to Paul Laybolt and Jenny Gimian for fact-checking related to all the people mentioned in the book; to Liam Phillips Lindsay for research, fact-checking, and overall fine-tuning; to John Sell for compiling the resources section; to Michal Keeley for her expert help in the final copyediting stage; and to Alan Kelly for rapid and accurate transcription of the many recorded conversations that formed the backbone of the book.

My family is a great source of support to me. I'm blessed by the unconditional love of my older brother and best friend, Al Ryan. He quit his job to run my first political campaign. His leadership brought us through the rough and tumble of Ohio politics and into Washington, giving me the platform from which to write this book. His wife, Carrie Ryan, and their children, Nicolas, Dominick, Andrea, and Antonio serve as examples of how magical life is if we just pay attention to the beauty that is right in front of us. I'm indebted to all my family in the Guerra and Rizzi clans. They've lifted me up throughout my life and were my original campaign team. I miss my aunts and uncles, who taught me the importance of family and the beauty of the Italian heritage: Rita and Fub Guerra, Phil and Emily Guerra, Fred and Mary Guerra, Pete and Rose DeChristopher, and Karen Guerra. Also, a special thanks to my dad, Papa Ryan, and Grandma Marcy for being the best grandparents. Thanks also to my aunt Maria and uncle Les, and my dear cousins Jeff and Michael Prudhomme, for their love, prayers, and concern, all too often from too many miles away.

A special thanks to all my friends and colleagues who work or have worked for the people of the 13th (formerly 17th) Congressional District in Ohio. Your service to the public in very difficult times inspires me. A special thanks to my friend and legislative director, Ryan Keating, for being such a savvy guy. Many of the thoughts articulated in this book result from years of our extended conversations. I'm indebted to all the teachers, coaches, nuns, priests, and brothers who taught me and my brother at Our Lady of Mount Carmel and John F. Kennedy High School. Especially Patrick Lowry, my government and religion teacher, who has worked for me for the past 10 years. Unselfish and gentle, he lives the New Testament. And Father Nick Arioli for being there for us during trying times and always reminding his students that they had hidden talent. Many thanks to my dear friend Father Ron Nuzzi. His embodiment of mindfulness and kindness always encourages me to look to the deeper side of life. He's the finest example of what it means to be a priest.

I'm grateful for the people of Northeast Ohio for allowing me to serve them as their representative. Their indomitable spirit, resiliency, and creativity are a source of pride for me and keep me optimistic about the future of our region. A special thanks to the people of Niles. I'm blessed to have been raised in a community that passes on the great traditions of the American melting pot. Thanks especially to Bill and Mary Ann Leonard, my second parents; Laurie Bretzinger and Jen Leonard, who are like sisters; and Grandma and Grandpa Gales. I've been blessed to have Ricky and Billy Leonard as next-door neighbors. Our values were shaped on baseball diamonds, football fields, and basketball courts together. They and their father helped me shape a sense of humor and an ability to laugh at myself and life's ironies—essential traits when practicing mindfulness. Rick is district director for all my Ohio offices. Few in the political world can match his skill and perceptiveness, and his commitment to our work gave me the opportunity to finish this project. Many thanks to Ron Grimes, Jerid Kurtz, and Crystal Patterson, all vital members of my Capitol Hill office, who provided a close reading of the original edition of this book at a critical stage.

I want to thank my wife, Andrea, for giving me the space, support, and encouragement needed to write this. And to our children—Mason, Bella, and Brady—for all the joy and laughs they gave me and the lessons they taught me. They fill my life with joy and laughter, and this book is my attempt to make this world a better place for them to live in.

I wrote this book predominantly on three-day writing retreats, so I wish to thank the friends who supplied their homes and gave of their time and effort to make that possible: To Bob and Amy Boyce, Michal Keeley and Jon Frank, and Jim and Carolyn Gimian. To Peter Good and Peter Volz, for helping us keep all the strands together. A special thanks to the now late Leo Keating for letting us use his chalet for a 10-day mindfulness and writing retreat that was essential to finishing the book. His generosity and life story have always been a personal inspiration to me.

Above all, I must thank my mother, Rochelle Ryan, for teaching me, by example, about love, loyalty, and the importance of faith. Her life exemplifies resiliency and dealing with life's tragedies with optimism and good cheer. I'm thankful for her unwavering confidence in me throughout the writing of this book and through the many ups and downs of life. And finally, as this book has illustrated many times, I am indebted to my grandparents John and Ann Guerra Rizzi. They were my first examples of how to live a mindful life.

ABOUT
THE AUTHOR

Tim Ryan was first elected to the U.S. House of Representatives in 2002, at the age of 29, and is currently serving in his eighth term representing Ohio's 13th Congressional District. He maintains a strong commitment to the economic and social well-being of his constituents in Northeast Ohio. He serves as a member of the House Armed Services Committee, as well as its subcommittees on Readiness and on Emerging Threats and Capabilities. He is also co-chairman of the Congressional Manufacturing Caucus.

Congressman Ryan follows a daily mindfulness practice. He has been an outspoken advocate for promoting mindfulness practice as an aid to dealing with the variety of complex problems facing the nation, and was instrumental in having mindfulness training included in the House of Representatives wellness program, starting in 2018. During his tenure in the House, he has helped to get mindfulness and social and emotional learning programs established in several schools in his district. He also spearheaded a conference at a medical school in his district on mindfulness-based stress reduction. Before being elected to Congress, Ryan served in the Ohio state senate, as president of the Trumbull County Young Democrats, as chairman of Earning by Learning in Warren, Ohio, and as a congressional aide.

Hay House Titles of Related Interest

YOU CAN HEAL YOUR LIFE, the movie,
starring Louise Hay & Friends
(available as a 1-DVD program, an expanded 2-DVD set,
and an online streaming video)
Learn more at www.hayhouse.com/louise-movie

THE SHIFT, the movie,
starring Dr. Wayne W. Dyer
(available as a 1-DVD program, an expanded 2-DVD set,
and an online streaming video)
Learn more at www.hayhouse.com/the-shift-movie

⌒

BE FEEL THINK DO: A Memoir, by Anne Bérubé, Ph.D.

MORE BEAUTIFUL THAN BEFORE: How Suffering Transforms Us,
by Steve Leder

*YOU HAVE 4 MINUTES TO CHANGE YOUR LIFE: Simple
4-Minute Meditations for Inspiration, Transformation, and True
Bliss,* by Rebekah Borucki

All of the above are available at your local bookstore,
or may be ordered by contacting Hay House (see next page).

⌒

We hope you enjoyed this Hay House book. If you'd like to receive our online catalog featuring additional information on Hay House books and products, or if you'd like to find out more about the Hay Foundation, please contact:

Hay House, Inc., P.O. Box 5100, Carlsbad, CA 92018-5100
(760) 431-7695 or (800) 654-5126
(760) 431-6948 (fax) or (800) 650-5115 (fax)
www.hayhouse.com® • www.hayfoundation.org

———

Published in Australia by:
Hay House Australia Pty. Ltd., 18/36 Ralph St., Alexandria NSW 2015
Phone: 612-9669-4299 • *Fax:* 612-9669-4144 • www.hayhouse.com.au

Published in the United Kingdom by:
Hay House UK, Ltd., Astley House, 33 Notting Hill Gate, London W11 3JQ
Phone: 44-20-3675-2450 • *Fax:* 44-20-3675-2451 • www.hayhouse.co.uk

Published in India by: Hay House Publishers India,
Muskaan Complex, Plot No. 3, B-2, Vasant Kunj, New Delhi 110 070
Phone: 91-11-4176-1620 • *Fax:* 91-11-4176-1630 • www.hayhouse.co.in

———

Access New Knowledge.
Anytime. Anywhere.

Learn and evolve at your own pace
with the world's leading experts.

www.hayhouseU.com

Hay House Podcasts
Bring Fresh, Free Inspiration Each Week!

Hay House proudly offers a selection of life-changing audio content via our most popular podcasts!

Hay House Meditations Podcast

Features your favorite Hay House authors guiding you through meditations designed to help you relax and rejuvenate. Take their words into your soul and cruise through the week!

Dr. Wayne W. Dyer Podcast

Discover the timeless wisdom of Dr. Wayne W. Dyer, world-renowned spiritual teacher and affectionately known as "the father of motivation." Each week brings some of the best selections from the 10-year span of Dr. Dyer's talk show on HayHouseRadio.com.

Hay House World Summit Podcast

Over 1 million people from 217 countries and territories participate in the massive online event known as the Hay House World Summit. This podcast offers weekly mini-lessons from World Summits past as a taste of what you can hear during the annual event, which occurs each May.

Hay House Radio Podcast

Listen to some of the best moments from HayHouseRadio.com, featuring expert authors such as Dr. Christiane Northrup, Anthony William, Caroline Myss, James Van Praagh, and Doreen Virtue discussing topics such as health, self-healing, motivation, spirituality, positive psychology, and personal development.

Hay House Live Podcast

Enjoy a selection of insightful and inspiring lectures from Hay House Live, an exciting event series that features Hay House authors and leading experts in the fields of alternative health, nutrition, intuitive medicine, success, and more! Feel the electricity of our authors engaging with a live audience, and get motivated to live your best life possible!

Find Hay House podcasts on iTunes, or visit
www.HayHouse.com/podcasts for more info.